Housetraining
FOR
DUMMIES®
2ND EDITION

by Susan McCullough

WILEY

Wiley Publishing, Inc.

Housetraining For Dummies®, 2nd Edition

Published by
Wiley Publishing, Inc.
111 River St.
Hoboken, NJ 07030-5774
www.wiley.com

About the Author

Susan McCullough writes about all things dog for print and online outlets all over the United States. She is a contributing editor to *Dog Fancy*, and her work has also appeared in the *AKC Gazette, AKC Family Dog, Your Dog,* the *Popular Dogs* magazine series, *Studio One Networks, The Washington Post,* and *Family Circle*. Her dog care books include *Senior Dogs For Dummies* and *Beagles For Dummies* (Wiley).

Susan is vice president of the Dog Writers Association of America (DWAA) and belongs to the Association of Pet Dog Trainers (APDT). She is a five-time winner of the DWAA's Maxwell Award for excellence in writing about dogs, and she also won the 2001 Eukanuba Canine Health Award for outstanding writing about canine health.

When she's not writing or hanging out with friends and family (both two-legged and four-legged), Susan counsels puzzled people on how to deal with canine potty problems and other dog-related quandaries. She lives in Vienna, Virginia, with her husband, Stan Chappell; their daughter, Julie Chappell (when Julie's on break from college); and the family's Golden Retriever, Allie.Visit Susan's Web site at www.susanmc.com and read her blog, *The Allie Chronicles*, at thealliechronicles.blogspot.com.

Dedication

For Allie, the dog I didn't know I needed

Author's Acknowledgments

Every book is a group effort, and this one is no exception. I want to thank everyone who made this book possible, including Tracy Boggier, Wiley acquisitions editor, who asked me to revisit housetraining, and Alissa Schwipps, Wiley senior project editor, who graciously made time in her crazy-busy schedule to do a literary three-peat with me. Thanks also to Patty Kovach, DVM, technical reviewer, whose expertise made this a better book; The Lunch Bunch — Victoria Schade, Pat Miller, Robin Bennett, Colleen Pelar, Penelope Brown, and Pam Wanveer — from whom I learn so much and have a great time doing so; and Windy Run's Allie McChappell, CGC (Canine Good Citizen), housetraining ace and the best office dog/ canine muse an author could have. And most of all, Stan Chappell, my husband, and Julie Chappell, my daughter, for being there for me when I've needed them (especially when I've taken unexpected bumps to the head) and for cheering me on the rest of the time.

Publisher's Acknowledgments

We're proud of this book; please send us your comments at http://dummies.custhelp.com. For other comments, please contact our Customer Care Department within the U.S. at 877-762-2974, outside the U.S. at 317-572-3993, or fax 317-572-4002.

Some of the people who helped bring this book to market include the following:

Acquisitions, Editorial, and Media Development

Senior Project Editor: Alissa Schwipps
(Previous Edition: Kelly Ewing)

Acquisitions Editor: Tracy Boggier

Senior Copy Editor: Danielle Voirol

Assistant Editor: Erin Calligan Mooney

Editorial Program Coordinator: Joe Niesen

Technical Editor: Patty Kovach, DVM

Senior Editorial Manager: Jennifer Ehrlich

Editorial Assistants: Jennette ElNaggar, David Lutton

Cover Photos: © GK Hart/ Vicki Hart

Cartoons: Rich Tennant
(www.the5thwave.com)

Composition Services

Project Coordinator: Katherine Crocker

Layout and Graphics: Reuben W. Davis, Christin Swinford

Special Art: Marcia Schlehr

Proofreaders: Cynthia Fields, John Greenough

Indexer: Potomac Indexing, LLC

Special Help

Amanda Gillum

Publishing and Editorial for Consumer Dummies

  Diane Graves Steele, Vice President and Publisher, Consumer Dummies

  Kristin Ferguson-Wagstaffe, Product Development Director, Consumer Dummies

  Ensley Eikenburg, Associate Publisher, Travel

  Kelly Regan, Editorial Director, Travel

Publishing for Technology Dummies

  Andy Cummings, Vice President and Publisher, Dummies Technology/General User

Composition Services

  Debbie Stailey, Director of Composition Services

Contents at a Glance

Table of Contents

Part II: Putting a Plan in Place 75

Chapter 5: Training to Love the Crate 77

Chapter 6: Heading to the Outside: Outdoor Housetraining.........................87

Chapter 7: Making Some Inside Moves: Indoor Housetraining 101

Introduction

When you brought home that adorable little puppy or noble-looking adult dog, you undoubtedly were looking forward to a lifetime of love, devotion, and companionship. Maybe you wanted a dog to jog with in the morning, have curl up at your feet in the evening, or talk to during the day. Perhaps you were looking forward to heaping lots of unconditional love upon a hard-luck rescue dog who hadn't known such love before. Or maybe you remembered watching *Lassie* when you were a kid and were hoping that your new family member could be the same sort of friend-of-a-lifetime that the famous Collie was for little Timmy.

Every new relationship between a person and a dog starts out with at least a little bit of fantasizing on the part of the person. Soon thereafter, though, reality intrudes upon those fantasies. All too often, that intrusion takes the form of a puddle or pile deposited on the floor of your home. The puddle is gross. The pile stinks. Both leave stains. And you are totally grossed out.

Loving a pooch who turns your nicely decorated home into a canine outhouse is tough. But this problem doesn't have to happen. You just need to teach your dog proper potty manners. In other words, you need to housetrain him.

When your dog is housetrained, both of your lives become a whole lot easier and immeasurably more satisfying. Gone are the doggie accidents, stains, and smells that keep professional carpet cleaners in business but all too often ruin the precious bonds between dogs and their people. I've written this book to make sure that you and your dog maintain those bonds.

About This Book

Housetraining For Dummies, 2nd Edition, is a reference book designed to help you not only teach your dog the ins and outs of basic bathroom behavior but also prevent your pooch from developing potty problems — or solve any problems she already has.

Whether you have a brand-new puppy who's piddling on your equally new Oriental rug; an unruly adolescent male dog who's practicing leg-lifts (and subsequent anointings) right next to your antique loveseat; a matronly female dog who's wetting her bed while she sleeps; or simply a pooch who never seems to know what he's supposed to do when you take him out, this book can help you sort out your dog's bathroom issues and resolve them, no matter what they are.

You don't have to read this book from start to finish to teach your canine companion proper potty deportment. If you want to know everything and then some about housetraining, begin reading here and plow through to the end. But if you have a specific concern, such as wanting to teach your dog to tell you when she needs to go out, skip the preliminaries, look over the table of contents, and proceed to the chapter that tells you exactly what you want to know.

Finally, this book is meant to be a guide but not a substitute for the up-close-and-personal advice that other experts such as veterinarians, trainers, and behaviorists give. If the suggestions here don't work for you and your dog, or if you have a question that this book doesn't cover, don't hesitate to contact any of these professionals.

Conventions Used in This Book

To help you find your way through this book — as in all *For Dummies* books — I've used the following conventions:

- *Italics* highlight new words and terms.
- **Boldfaced** text indicates the actions in numbered steps and keywords in bulleted lists.
- Monofont indicates a Web address.

In addition, I've added some conventions of my own. For one thing, I'm not even going to try to sound genteel in this book — after all, you're dealing with bodily waste here. That's why I refer to canine bodily byproducts as *poop* and *pee* — although I occasionally substitute other terms just for the sake of variety.

At the same time, I refrain from using other terms commonly employed in discussions of pooch potty protocol. Specifically, I don't use the words *housebreak, housebreaking,* or *housebroken* anywhere in this book, except when I describe the history of canine toilet training. That's because when you teach your dogs to eliminate appropriately, you're not breaking anything. In fact, you're doing quite the opposite: By teaching the dog to poop and pee when and where you want him to, you're building bonds between you two. You're laying the foundation for a loving, long-lasting relationship.

Finally, there's the matter of gender. Many writers like to refer to canine companions in gender-neutral terms such as *it* unless discussing a specific dog, such as Daisy or Max. But I don't agree with them. Any dog, even if spayed or neutered, has a clear gender. More importantly, every dog is a living being who deserves the dignity of being referred to as such. For that reason, I use the word *who,* not *that,* along with *he, she, him, her, his,* and *hers* to refer to canine companions. I tend to alternate the genders of the example dogs in a chapter, so any of those pronouns (or a name such as Fido or Lassie) applies to dogs of either gender unless I indicate otherwise.

What You're Not to Read

I'd be thrilled if you were to read every word of this book, but I know better. You're like me: way too busy, with far too little time to accomplish everything on your daily to-do list. Plus, you want to know as soon as possible how to keep your floors and furniture from becoming a doggie latrine. To help you differentiate between what you need to know and what you can do without, I've made the do-without stuff easy for you to spot. That stuff includes the following:

- ✔ **Sidebars:** These shaded boxes contain anecdotes or interesting bits of information that can make housetraining easier and more effective, but if you skip them and apply the suggestions in the main text, you'll still have a pooch who knows when and where he's supposed to potty.

- ✔ **Text next to the Technical Stuff icon:** Information located next to this icon is interesting, but it may go into far more detail about housetraining than you need for teaching your dog her bathroom basics.

- ✔ **Legal stuff:** Otherwise known as the material on the copyright page, the text here is of interest mainly to Wiley's legal eagles. Even if you're interested in copyright law, I guarantee that you can find more information on the subject elsewhere.

Foolish Assumptions

I've written this book assuming that one of the following scenarios applies to you and your dog:

✔ You're about to get a new puppy — or have just gotten one — and want to teach her proper potty protocol as quickly and effectively as possible.

✔ Your puppy or adult dog has never quite mastered that protocol, and you want to know how to transform him from bathroom bungler to housetraining ace.

✔ Your once well-housetrained dog appears to have developed some bathroom issues, and you want to know how to solve those problems instead of just having to live with them.

If you and your canine companion fit into any of the preceding categories, this book is for you.

How This Book Is Organized

This book can give you the full scoop on making the housetraining process as hassle-free as possible. If you read any part of *Housetraining For Dummies*, you can gain valuable insights on how to teach your puppy or adult dog to do his business where and when you want him to. Here's how I've organized the book to help you do just that.

Part 1: Preparing to Potty Train Your Pooch

Before you can housetrain your hound, you need to get yourself ready to do so. Therefore, this part explains the basic principles of canine learning in general and of housetraining in particular. Here, too, is where you get the info you need to decide where you want your dog's bathroom to be: inside or outside your home. You also get the lowdown on what equipment you need to teach your dog proper potty protocol. Finally, you discover how not only to jump-start your dog's housetraining progress but also to give her a leg up on lifelong good health by feeding her the right kinds of foods.

Part II: Putting a Plan in Place

Now that you've made some basic decisions, gotten a primer on housetraining theory, acquired the right housetraining gear, and stocked up on gourmet doggie fare, you're ready to start the housetraining process in earnest. Part II tells you all you need to know to turn your housetrainee into a housetraining graduate, whether you opt for indoor training or choose to have your pooch potty in the great outdoors. You also discover some techniques that can make managing your dog's bathroom maneuvers infinitely easier and determine when you can consider your hound a true housetraining ace.

Part III: Solving Housetraining Problems

Alas, even the solidly housetrained dog can acquire potty problems. Some of those problems require remedial housetraining, others may actually be signs of illness, and still others may reflect human mistakes, not the dog's. Part III helps you determine what kind of problem your dog really has (and that problem, for some dogs, is simply that they're very small) and what you need to do to solve it.

Part IV: The Part of Tens

Part IV is where I introduce some top-ten lists and have even more fun discussing housetraining than I do in the preceding three parts. In the process, I emphasize some important housetraining principles. And if, for some reason, you're wondering whether housetraining is worth the trouble, this part — specifically Chapter 13 — gives you the incentive you need to keep plugging away.

Appendix

If you're interested in getting more information about housetraining and other aspects of dog care, I've included an appendix full of resources after Chapter 13.

Icons Used in This Book

To make this book simpler to use, I've included some icons to help you find and fathom key ideas and information.

This icon calls attention to time- and hassle-saving ideas or items that are especially helpful when housetraining your dog.

This icon denotes information that's so critical to successful housetraining that you should read it more than once — just to ensure that you remember it as you potty-train your own pooch.

This icon flags dangers to your dog's well-being. It also lets you know when an apparent housetraining problem is really a medical problem that demands a veterinarian's attention.

Perhaps you want the full scoop on why dens are such a big part of most dogs' lives or how dogs use their pee to communicate with each other. This icon flags such nonessential information for you. On the other hand, if you just want to understand the basic concepts of housetraining, sidestep this icon and move on.

Where to Go From Here

If you haven't acquired your dog yet, or if she's just arrived, reading from the very beginning of this book and working your way through to the end is best. But if your canine companion has been with you for a while, or if you're just trying to solve a particular pooch potty problem, don't fret. Head to the table of contents or to the index, where you can find the topic that can help solve your dog's specific housetraining problems.

Part I

Preparing to Potty Train Your Pooch

The 5th Wave   By Rich Tennant

"We've trained him to 'go on command.' Currently, the command is, 'RALPH- GRAB THE DOG BEFORE HE GOES ON THE CARPET!'"

In this part...

*B*efore you can housetrain your dog, you need to
prepare yourself for the task. In this part, you find
out how to do just that, starting with understanding
exactly what housetraining is. From there, you discover
the importance of working with your dog's instincts to
teach him basic bathroom manners, and you get some
help deciding where your dog's bathroom should be,
whether indoors or outdoors. Finally, you get a shopping
list of what you need to housetrain your hound effectively
and of what to feed him so you not only make the housetraining process easier but also safeguard his overall
health and well-being.

Chapter 1

No, Virginia, It's Not That Hard: Understanding Housetraining Basics

Max, a 10-week-old Beagle, is delighting his new owner with his puppy antics but is dismaying her with his penchant for peeing all over her recently installed carpet. No matter how recently he tinkled outside, he always seems to have something left over with which to tinkle on the floor covering.

Allie, a 6-year-old Golden Retriever, would never pee on anyone's carpet. Her people can count on her to do her business three or four times a day: first thing in the morning, early in the afternoon, in the late afternoon (sometimes), and in the evening before she retires for the night. On the rare occasions that she needs an extra bathroom break, she lets her people know by heading to the back door and scratching it — or if her tummy is giving her trouble, by waking up one of her people to get her outside in time to avoid an accident.

Cody, a 3-year-old Chihuahua, can hold his water pretty well — sometimes. Other times, though, he seems to suffer from bathroom-manners amnesia or a sudden preference for taking a whiz any place except where he's supposed to.

Which of these dogs is housetrained? Which ones aren't? In this chapter, you not only find the answer to those two questions but also discover why housetraining plays such an important role in whether you and your dog can live happily ever after.

What Housetraining Is — and Why It Matters

To know whether your dog is really housetrained, you need to understand exactly what housetraining is. Unfortunately, most dictionaries aren't all that helpful here. For example, the *Random House Dictionary* offers a two-word definition: "to housebreak." That doesn't tell you much — after all, you're not teaching your dog to break anything! The *American Heritage Dictionary* offers the same terse definition, although it does add that the term is primarily British.

No matter where the term *housetraining* originates, defining it still requires precision and directness. Simply put, *housetraining* is the process in which you teach your dog to eliminate when you want him to and where you want him to — and to refrain from eliminating at any other time or place.

That definition doesn't allow much room for errors or lapses. And clearly, when measured against those criteria, a dog who consistently does his duty outdoors or in a designated indoor area is fully housetrained. That's not the case, though, with a dog who usually tinkles outdoors, never tinkles outdoors, or only occasionally tinkles outdoors (or performs with similar levels of consistency in a predetermined indoor Bowser bathroom). Housetraining is one of those all-or-nothing cases. That being the case, Allie is the only dog in the chapter intro who you can consider truly housetrained.

Why does such precision matter? Simple: An otherwise well-behaved, healthy dog who doesn't know proper pooch potty protocol is much more likely to lose her home than a similar dog who knows her bathroom basics. No human being likes to have his home turned into a multiroom canine toilet — and if such a human can't teach his dog to take her bathroom business elsewhere, that dog is likely to find herself going elsewhere.

Why Your Dog Can't Be "a Little Bit Housetrained"

Housetraining is an either-or proposition: Either a dog is house-trained, or she isn't. To say that a dog is "partially trained" or "a little bit housetrained" is like saying that a woman is "partially pregnant" or "a little bit pregnant." None of those terms compute.

If you consider your dog to be "a little bit housetrained," you're really saying that he hasn't completely learned proper bathroom manners yet. That means you can't really rely on him to go to the bathroom only where and when you want him to.

Until your dog is totally housetrained, you always face the chance that Lassie will decide to use your brand new area rug as her toilet or that Laddie will choose to anoint your mother-in-law's prized Chippendale chair. And of course, for some dogs, especially puppies, those chances are way better than even. That's certainly the case with Max, the young Beagle from the chapter intro who's been using that new carpet as his own personal potty.

But owners of adult dogs like Cody, the Chihuahua who's occasionally leaving unwelcome puddles throughout his owner's abode, also cope with unreliable canines. Cody appears to have forgotten the lessons in bathroom manners his owners taught him years ago — or perhaps he never quite understood those lessons in the first place. Chapter 9 describes typical cases of pooches who appear to have forgotten the fine art of proper canine bathroom behavior. Or maybe Cody doesn't feel well. Chapter 10 focuses on why a pooch may pee or poop inappropriately — and what owners can do to solve such problems.

But for now, it's fair to say that although housetraining is an either-or proposition, there's definitely more than one way to teach a dog proper potty behavior. Before you start, though, you need to get yourself and your household ready for the task. Chapter 2 helps you prepare by giving you a primer on canine instincts and on how to capitalize on those instincts to help your dog become a happy housetrainee. Chapter 3 focuses on equipping you, your home, and your dog to ensure housetraining success. And Chapter 4 hones in on a crucial component of the housetraining process: food. After all, what goes in your dog must eventually come out, in one form or another!

Exploring Housetraining Methods

Most people who choose to live with dogs want to be able to regulate their canines' bathroom deportment. They want their dogs to poop and pee where and when *they* (the people) choose.

Fortunately, you can choose between two methods designed to help you achieve this goal. The right choice for you and your dog depends on many factors, some of which relate less to your dog's needs than to your way of living. In this section, I discuss indoor and outdoor training and talk about some of the lifestyle issues that may help you choose one method over another.

Location, location, location: Outdoor versus indoor training

The two housetraining methods I discuss in this book are all about location — as in where you want your pooch to potty: indoors or outdoors.

Outdoor training

If the idea of turning part of your house into a canine bathroom doesn't thrill you, you're far from alone. That same lack of enthusiasm is probably the primary reason that millions of dog owners train their four-legged friends to do their bathroom business outside. *Outdoor training* involves teaching a dog to eliminate in a potty area located outside your home. The potty area can be a designated spot in your backyard or wherever you allow your dog to do his business.

Outdoor training has plenty of advantages. First and foremost, as soon as your dog knows what he's supposed to do and where he's supposed to do it, you never again need to worry about canine waste marring your floors, staining your carpets, or otherwise stinking up your house. You also have more floor space to use and enjoy, because you don't have any newspapers, litter boxes, or other indoor canine bathroom paraphernalia to get in the way of household foot traffic. Finally, those who choose to walk their dogs outdoors can get some healthful, enjoyable exercise as well as some special bonding time with their canine companions. If these advantages appeal to you, head over to Chapter 6, which gives you the straight scoop on teaching your pooch to potty outside.

But outdoor training carries some disadvantages, too — just ask anyone who's had to go outside with his pooch on a cold or rainy night. Fortunately, a little extra training can go a long way toward alleviating the problem of the pooch who takes too long to do his business during bad weather. Chapter 8 offers ideas on how to teach your dog to become a proactive housetraining graduate and provides some hints on how to help your housetrainee expedite his excretions.

Don't think that letting your pooch potty in your yard relieves you of the obligation to clean up those deposits. Unless you like having bright yellow patches in the middle of your green grass (a problem I address in Chapter 3) or stepping in the other stuff — because that stuff generally doesn't degrade fast enough for you to totally avoid such missteps — plan on cleaning up after your four-legged friend even if his potty is on your property.

Indoor training

Indoor training involves teaching a dog to eliminate in a potty area located inside your home. The potty area can be some newspapers spread on the floor in one room, a litter box tucked discreetly into a corner, or some other device located in a designated area of your abode.

A dog who's indoor-trained makes a beeline for that indoor location whenever he feels the urge to eliminate. As soon as he's finished, cleanup is easy: You just flush the poop down the toilet and either throw away or clean the surface upon which the poop or pee landed.

Indoor training is a viable housetraining option if, for some reason, taking your dog outside to eliminate isn't practical. It's also worth trying if your adult dog and his waste byproducts are very small.

But indoor training carries some disadvantages. It's impractical if your dog is much bigger than toy-sized (consider how big that waste is likely to be). Moreover, if your canine companion is male, sooner or later he'll probably starting lifting his leg when he pees. When that happens, his ability to aim accurately may decline. Instead of hitting the litter box, newspaper, or other toilet, he may leave a stinky puddle on your floor.

Either way, if you decide that indoor training is right for you and your dog, mosey on over the Chapter 7. There, you get the lowdown on how to get your four-legged friend to squat down in the proper indoor location.

Looking at lifestyle factors to help you choose your method

How do you decide which housetraining method works best for you? The right answer depends as much on your way of living as it does on your dog's needs.

Maybe you're one of those lucky people who not only work from home during the day but also have some nice outdoor places to walk to. For you, walking a dog can be a real pleasure — and at times even a sanity saver. A housetraining method that takes you and your dog outdoors is probably an attractive option.

Perhaps, though, you're an elderly person or a mobility-impaired individual who can't get out and around easily. The dog walk that's pure pleasure for your work-at-home neighbor may be pure torture for you. If this description fits you, the ideal housetraining method probably means never having to leave the house. Indoor training may be a better choice.

Or perhaps you live in a high-rise apartment building in the middle of the city. When your canine companion needs a potty break, you can't just snap on the leash, open the front door, and head out for a quick stroll or a trip to a designated doggie toilet area. Instead, your route to the great outdoors may require you and your dog to walk to the opposite end of a long hallway, wait for the elevator to stop at your floor, ride down to your building lobby on the elevator, and finally get yourselves to the proper spot outside. And all this time, your dog is expected to hold her water. If you and your dog face such obstacles *en route* to an outdoor bathroom, you may also want to consider keeping her potty indoors.

Those are just a few examples of how your lifestyle can affect the housetraining method you select for your four-legged friend. No matter which method you choose, this book gives you detailed instructions on how to housetrain your dog.

Surviving Setbacks and Special Situations

Although housetraining is generally a straightforward process, chances are you'll encounter setbacks during the training period. And even when your four-legged friend becomes a housetraining graduate, he's bound to do some occasional backsliding. In any case, you'll likely see situations in which your consistently rock-solid housetrainee suddenly seems to lose his edge, and neither you nor he knows why.

For setbacks during the housetraining period, Chapters 6 and 7 offer guides for troubleshooting bathroom errors. In those chapters, you find questions that can help you determine the mistakes you made that led to that unauthorized puddle or pile (and yes, during this period, generally any doggie accidents result from your mistakes).

Post-housetraining backsliding can be a little more complicated, but here, too, help is at hand. Although every dog is an individual, almost every healthy housetraining-challenged dog fits one of ten broad profiles. Chapter 9 describes these profiles in detail and outlines options so you can either help your dog overcome her housetraining challenges or, in a few cases, live with your dog and her disabilities.

That said, a lot of apparently housetraining-challenged dogs really don't have bathroom issues at all: Instead, they're feeling under the weather. Some of the maladies that result in doggie bathroom lapses are minor, and others aren't. Chapter 10 lists some of the most common bathroom-related symptoms, suggests possible causes of those symptoms, and recommends steps to take.

Understanding the Role You and Your Family Play

Most dog trainers say that the most important part of their jobs isn't training dogs — it's training the humans to train the dogs. In Chapter 12, you discover the ten most common human housetraining hang-ups and how to prevent them.

You and the other humans in your life play crucial roles in your dog's housetraining progress and ultimate success (or lack thereof). Not only do you teach your dog the ins and outs of proper potty protocol, but you also create the conditions that can make or break a housetraining program. For one thing, house-training needs to be a family affair. Here's why:

> ✔ **To keep the diet consistent:** No matter how diligently you're trying to regulate Sparky's bathroom urges by regulating the kind and amount of food you feed him, such diligence is all for naught if your partner or child is sneaking the dog snacks all the while.

> ✔ **To help you avoid burnout:** Housetraining can be pretty simple, but it can also be pretty tedious when just one person is doing the day-in, day-out routine of feeding, walking, and confining the housetrainee.

Chapter 11 helps you get all the humans in your household, including the kids, on the same page so you can all housetrain Sparky together.

But maybe getting your family on board isn't your problem. Maybe you're trying to deal with housetraining a dog while working away from home all day. Even well into the 21st century, corporate America still isn't all that great about accommodating the needs of employees' family members, whether those members are human or canine. Chapter 11 offers suggestions on how to give your housetrainee some daytime relief and still keep your job.

The same chapter also covers coping strategies for other special situations, such as traveling with a dog you're trying to housetrain or even just providing for the bathroom needs of a housetraining graduate while you're on the road.

Your dog or puppy has all the instincts and desire he needs to motivate him to acquire good bathroom manners — he just needs you to get him going. Do the job right, and not only will your dog become a housetraining ace, but the two of you will build a bond that goes the distance for years to come.

Chapter 2

Training the Housetrainer: Taking the Right Approach

*B*efore a person can teach any subject, he or she has to know not only the subject itself but also how to convey that information to a student. That's just as true for housetraining as it is for any other topic. For your puppy or dog to learn basic bathroom manners, you need to teach him those manners in a way he can understand.

That said, your four-legged friend brings plenty of positive attributes to the housetraining process: a strong instinct to seek out a den, an equally strong instinct to keep that den clean, an ability to learn through repetition, and a desire to score rewards. But it's up to you to capitalize on those attributes and develop an approach to housetraining that enables him to get the hang of proper potty protocol with minimum stress on him — and on you.

A lot of what I talk about in this chapter may seem to range far afield from the task at hand: teaching your dog where and when to eliminate. But nothing could be further from the truth, because housetraining is probably one of the first lessons — if not *the* first lesson — you'll try to teach your dog.

The way you try to show your dog proper potty protocol lays the foundation for your efforts to teach him other maneuvers, such as coming when called, sitting when told to, and walking nicely while leashed. What you do now, in this most basic of lessons, can set the tone for your relationship with your dog in the years ahead. For that reason alone, it's worth taking the time to do the job well.

Leaving Behind Housetraining Methods of Yesteryear

Housetraining a dog doesn't have to be difficult. But a generation ago, not many people realized that. At best, housetraining was a difficult undertaking; at worst, it was a total failure. Unfortunately, failures occurred all too often.

Here's what may have been behind these failures. Mom (she was the one who usually got stuck with the housetraining task) would see a puddle or pile of poop on the floor. She'd freak — naturally, the little deposit would be gracing a just-mopped kitchen floor or freshly shampooed living room carpet — and go on the warpath to find the canine culprit. When she found him, she'd grab the culprit by the collar, drag him over to the puddle or pile, and yell, "Bad dog!" at him. Maybe she'd swat him with a rolled-up newspaper. She may even have rubbed his nose in the object of his offense. The terrified pooch would then creep away, and things would settle down, at least temporarily.

Maybe the dog would eventually figure out what Mom was trying to tell him. Often, though, he wouldn't. And so the dog would soon have another accident, and the whole miserable cycle would begin again. Still, the dog was learning something: He learned that he should avoid the rolled-up newspaper at all costs. He also learned that he should avoid screaming moms.

Most of the problems people had with potty training their dogs weren't the dogs' faults; they were the people's faults. People knew very little about the canine instincts that make housetraining and other training easier. They knew only that they didn't want their dogs to do their business inside the house.

Since then, dog trainers and owners alike have discovered a lot about how dogs learn. And you can use that knowledge to make housetraining a much easier process than when your mother was trying to do the job.

Using Your Pooch's Instincts to Lay a Foundation

When housetraining your pooch, you're not working with a blank slate. Your canine companion probably learned a lot about bathroom behavior before you ever met her — whether she came to you as a puppy or as an adult dog. And a lot of what she knows comes from her *instincts:* those feelings, drives, and desires that have been with your dog since the moment she was born. They're hard-wired into her very being. No one taught her the behaviors that result from these impulses; they just came naturally.

The places where your dog chooses to sleep, her tendency to hoard things, her love of licking your face, her delight in fetching objects — these and countless other actions and reactions may all be inborn. And although some of these instincts don't affect her ability to be housetrained, others do. After you find out about some of these inborn impulses, you can begin to direct them in ways that help your dog learn to do what you want her to do. Your dog's instincts help her pick up not only potty deportment but also just about anything else you want your dog to know.

The training your dog has already had

You can housetrain almost any dog, but the challenges of teaching a puppy to go potty may differ from those you encounter when you try to teach the same maneuvers to an adult dog. Some of that has to do with the kind of nurturing and training the dog has already received.

The wee ones: Preliminary training and physical limits

All a healthy puppy usually needs to become housetrained is some time to grow and to develop some self-control — and of course, some guidance from you in the meantime.

If you got your puppy from a reputable breeder, Fifi may already know the rudiments of proper potty behavior. After all, the well-bred pup has had lots of opportunities to learn about keeping clean and getting along with other dogs (and people) — both of which are important prehousetraining skills. A puppy who has nailed those basics is easier to teach than one who lacks such knowledge.

Many breeders go even further. They take their puppies outside every morning and after meals, and they praise the little pups when they eliminate. If your puppy's breeder did that (ask when you're interviewing prospective breeders), he or she already did some of your dog's housetraining for you. The same may be true of a dog you adopt from a shelter, rescue group, or individual.

But even if your new puppy aced those preliminary lessons, one crucial lesson she's only just starting to learn is the lesson of self-control. To put it simply, your little pup just can't hold it — at least not for very long. A puppy younger than 4 months doesn't have a big enough bladder or sufficient muscle control to go more than a couple of hours without eliminating. As she gets older, a pup's ability to control herself gradually increases. By the time she reaches adulthood at about 1 year of age, a healthy dog usually has plenty of self-control. In fact, some adult dogs can hold it for a *very* long time.

Grown-up pooches: Unlearning bad habits

Even an adult dog who appears to have an iron bladder isn't necessarily housetrained. The fact that she can hold it doesn't necessarily mean that she will hold it. An adult dog may be burdened with mental baggage or just plain bad habits that can create additional obstacles to housetraining.

For example, if you adopted your young adult dog from an animal shelter, her previous owners may not have bothered to housetrain her — or if they did, they may have done a poor job. Either way, her failure to master proper potty deportment may well have been what landed her in the shelter in the first place.

Some shelter and rescue dogs have behavioral problems that manifest themselves as inappropriate elimination — for example, a shy dog may roll over and pee whenever someone stands above her and looks directly at her. Even a dog who's been a model of proper bathroom behavior at one point in her life can later appear to forget what she's been taught.

Not surprisingly, then, housetraining an adult dog is often less straightforward than housetraining a puppy. The grown-up pooch who has less-than-stellar bathroom manners often needs to unlearn some bad but well-entrenched habits before learning new ones. The person who lives with such a dog may need to develop his detective skills and figure out why his canine companion keeps making bathroom mistakes.

In any case, though, when you know something about your canine friend's instincts and impulses, you have a leg up on your efforts to housetrain her.

Learning from his mom

Even while he's still with his litter, a puppy is learning a lot about life as a dog. From his littermates, he learns not to bite too hard (if he bites at all) and how to jockey for position among his brothers and sisters at feeding time. And he learns a lot about proper bathroom behavior, too.

How long can a dog hold it?

Some dogs appear to have bladders made of iron. My late, great Sheltie, Cory, was one such canine. When the weather was bad, he slapped his floodgates shut. His personal best was a whopping 23 hours, even though my family and I gave him ample opportunity to unload during that time period.

Still, just because your dog has an iron bladder doesn't mean you should put it to the test. Here are some guidelines:

✔ Most experts say a dog needs a chance to pee at least every eight to ten hours.

✔ For puppies, the standard guideline is that they can hold it for the number of months they've lived plus one. In other words, your 3-month-old youngster can hold it for about four hours, max. But for many puppies of that age, even four hours is pushing their anatomical limits; they may need trips every three hours or even every two hours for a while. My current canine companion, Allie the Golden Retriever, was one such puppy.

✔ Very small puppies, such as toy breeds, often need hourly potty breaks when they're under 4 months of age simply because their bladders are so small.

Chapters 6 and 7 address scheduling potty breaks in detail.

Puppies can start learning elimination etiquette from the time they're about 3 or 4 weeks old or in some cases, even earlier. Generally, their bathroom manners start kicking in when they have sufficient motor skills to start wandering around the whelping box where they've been living with their mom and perhaps outside the box, too.

The mama dog takes advantage of this ability. When the pups indicate they're about to go potty, she may use her nose to push them outside the box if they haven't already gotten themselves out of there. Doing so keeps their poop and pee from stinking up the doggie domicile. If the mama dog and puppies are lucky enough to be residing in the home of a good breeder, several layers of newspaper will be at the other end of the box or other quarters for the puppies to eliminate on. After the puppies eliminate on the newspaper that the breeder placed on the floor for just that purpose, she whisks the soiled papers away and replaces them with fresh ones. Those are ways a breeder reinforces the mama dog's efforts.

By 7 or 8 weeks of age, most puppies have developed enough control to master this first bathroom lesson. They have to poop and pee every couple of hours or so, but they've learned to listen to their bodies, and they can tell when they need to go. When they get those urges, they try to scurry away from their den before giving in to that compulsion to squat. This effort to eliminate away from the den signals that a puppy is ready to begin learning the rudiments of housetraining.

Denning dynamics

The lessons a puppy learns about keeping clean go way beyond what her mom makes her do (see the preceding section). The nest that a dog's mother teaches her to help keep clean is really her first den — and dens are a big deal in the lives of most dogs.

For a dog, the den is simply an area that she can call her own. Generally, it's a small place that's at least somewhat enclosed on two or three sides but is also open on at least one side. The area may be dark, but it doesn't have to be. What it *does* have to be is a place where the dog feels safe and secure.

Unlike her wolf ancestors, the domestic dog doesn't need a den to ensure her physical survival, but her urge to find a den is still very strong (see Figure 2-1). My Golden Retriever office-mate, Allie, is a case in point — see the nearby sidebar titled "The under-dog: Improvising dens."

Figure 2-1: Dogs can find dens in unexpected places.

The under-dog: Improvising dens

My Golden Retriever Allie is using one of her dens right now. While I've been typing this chapter at the computer atop my desk, she came into my office and crept under that desk. She's now lying at my feet, protected on two sides by the walls of my office and on a third side by a part of the desk. My legs provide a kind of doorway that hides her from the view of others who come into the room. However, she still has a clear view of anyone else who comes in.

The desk isn't the only den available to Allie, though. She also enjoys napping under other tables in the house while my family and I are nearby. And sometimes, while the rest of our family is watching TV, my Golden girl spends some time in the dog crate she's had since she was a puppy. She also makes a beeline for the crate whenever she sees me wielding the vacuum cleaner, against which she appears to harbor some apprehensions. Inside that crate, Allie waits calmly, knowing that she's safe and secure, while I wage another battle in my never-ending war against dust bunnies.

Cleanliness is next to dog-liness

So-called dog people — humans who are enamored of anything and everything remotely canine — like to say that the word *God* is really *dog* spelled backward. They may espouse the motto of a magazine called *The Bark*: "Dog is my co-pilot." These dog people aren't being blasphemous. But their juxtaposition of *God* and *dog* has interesting implications for housetraining. Although many people believe that "cleanliness is next to godliness," most dogs instinctively adhere to the notion that cleanliness is next to dog-liness. In other words, dogs instinctively want to keep themselves clean.

Sometimes a dog's definition of cleanliness differs slightly from yours. You probably don't like the idea of Fido's splashing in a mud puddle, but Fido may not mind the mud at all. In terms of peeing and pooping, though, Fido and most of his canine compatriots draw the line between dirt and cleanliness — and they draw that line right smack in front of their dens.

Instinctively, a normal, healthy dog will do just about anything to avoid having to use his den as a toilet area. The last thing he wants to do is deposit his bodily waste anywhere near his cherished domicile. You can make that impulse work in your favor as you housetrain your dog. The impulse to keep the den clean is the cornerstone to teaching dogs to poop and pee only where and when you want them to. The drive to use a den and the drive to avoid soiling that den form the basis of easy, effective housetraining using a crate.

Life without guilt

Suppose that your dog makes a mistake. Say that she anoints your freshly mopped kitchen floor or leaves a little pile of poop in the foyer. Do you think she feels bad about it? Do you think she's overcome with remorse? Do you think she even remembers she's done a dirty deed within five minutes of committing the act? The answers to those questions are no, no, and no. Guilt and remorse aren't in your dog's emotional repertoire.

"Now, wait a minute," you say. "When I come home at night from work and see that Fido's peed on the rug, he sure looks to me as though he's feeling guilty. And when I start yelling at him, his ears go back, his tail goes between his legs, and he kind of cringes. He *knows* he's done something wrong."

Fido knows something all right — but that something isn't any realization that he's messed up big time. What he does know is that you're angry. If you're yelling his name, he also figures out pretty quickly that you're angry at *him*. But he doesn't have a clue as to why you're so upset; he's long since forgotten about his little rug-christening party. All he knows is that you're mad at him, and he's scared of you. Under such circumstances, he takes what looks to him like two prudent courses of action: literally making himself smaller (that's why he cringes) and beating a hasty retreat.

Does he understand that you don't want him to have any more accidents in the house? Nope. Does he realize that if he didn't have any accidents, you wouldn't become angry? No, again. He's just doing everything he can to minimize your wrath and, when that fails, to get away from that wrath — and from you.

Your dog lives a life that's completely free of guilt. He doesn't connect one of his long-ago actions with the angry outburst you're having now, which is why yelling at your dog after the fact doesn't teach him anything except to be afraid of you. Time, patience, and consistency are much more likely to get you the results you seek.

Learning by repetition

Your dog's inability to remember past mistakes doesn't mean that she can't make connections. On the contrary, she's very good at linking cause and effect. You can use that linking ability to teach her proper bathroom behavior or just about anything else you want her to know. How? Behold the power of repetition.

In fact, many times your dog learns something that you didn't plan to teach her. For example, my Golden Retriever, Allie, knows when I'm about to leave the house — and in response to my near departure, she often heads down to her crate on her own. Figuring out how she knew when I was leaving took me a while, but then I realized that I perform the same sequence of actions every time I leave the house: I put on some lipstick, pick up my purse, and get out my car keys. That sequence sends Allie to her crate.

Although repetition is the key to teaching your dog what you want her to know, you can do less repeating when you provide her with some sort of incentive for doing the right thing. Find out more about this positive approach in the later section titled "Rewarding the good, ignoring the goofs."

The need for attachment

Ever see a litter of young puppies? They tumble over each other constantly and seem to be touching each other all the time. Rarely do you see one puppy consistently go off by himself. Puppies need each other for warmth and companionship; they thrive in each other's company.

But perhaps when you welcomed home your new puppy or dog, you made the mistake of having him sleep by himself in the kitchen or basement. If so, you undoubtedly experienced a night full of heart-rending wails, yips, and howls. Your canine companion didn't like being alone, away from his littermates or the companions of his previous home. Being away from *you* made those already bad feelings seem even worse.

And of course, you know about the neighborhood dog whose owner leaves him alone in the backyard all day, every day, and who barks his head off — much to the annoyance of those who live nearby. Why does he do it? Boredom is one reason. Loneliness is another.

 Dogs are social animals. When they have a chance to choose between being alone and being with another individual, they generally choose the latter.

What does this need for company have to do with housetraining? Plenty. Not only does your dog's desire to be with you help build a precious bond between the two of you, but it also helps you keep track of where he is and what he's doing during the housetraining process. No matter how you look at it, your dog's instinctive desire to be close to you is something you can use as part of his housetraining — and any other training, for that matter.

How instincts can be thwarted

Instincts play a big role in how quickly your dog masters the art of housetraining. Many puppies learn basic cleanliness and social skills — two important prehousetraining accomplishments — from their mothers and littermates. But what if, for some reason, a puppy doesn't pick up those lessons in the first few weeks of her life? And how can that happen? One answer to how that happens is just two words: puppy mills.

Puppy mills: Inhibiting instincts

Puppy mills are substandard breeding operations in which female dogs are forced to mate as often as possible. Breeders raise mother and pups in deplorable conditions: I'm talking tiny cages in which these poor animals barely have enough room to turn around. They also often have to live knee-deep in their own poop and pee.

Having to live in her own filth is a surefire way to short-circuit a dog's instinctive drive to do her bathroom business away from her den. She can't get away from her den. And especially if she's a puppy, she can't hold it forever. Sooner or later, she has to go, and if the den is the only place where she can eliminate, that's where she does so. Eventually, she learns to deal with it.

What does this kind of situation mean for housetraining? Simple: A puppy-mill dog may take quite a while to recover her instinct to potty away from her den. And until she does, housetraining will be extremely difficult for everyone involved. This doesn't mean that a puppy-mill pooch can't be housetrained. Plenty of people have persevered until their canine companions finally understood where and when they were supposed to potty. But getting to that point takes lots of time and even more patience.

Unfortunately, many people lack such patience. When such patience is absent, life with their puppy-mill potty delinquents may veer off in one of two directions. Either the owners put up with a dog they say is "partially housetrained" (which really means the dog isn't housetrained at all), or the owners decide that they can't tolerate the stains, smells, and aggravation of a dog who can't learn basic bathroom manners. In turn, they either relegate the dog to remote areas of the house or, worse, get rid of the dog. Any way you look at it, the outcome is unhappy for all concerned.

Clearly, avoiding such problems in the first place is a good idea. How? By not buying a puppy or dog who comes from a puppy mill. A large number of these pooches end up in retail pet stores, such as those located in shopping malls. Others are sold by dealers who pose as breeders and advertise online or through print classifieds.

You can evaluate a breeder by visiting the premises, asking to see the mama dog, and using the guidelines in the nearby "What is a reputable breeder?" sidebar.

Many pet stores have stopped selling puppies themselves and instead hold adoption events to allow shelters and rescue groups to showcase the puppies and dogs who need new homes. Such stores clearly indicate that they're holding such events, and personnel from the shelter or rescue group are there to talk with you about the animals up for adoption. If that's the case with the pet store you're considering, assess the puppies and dogs up for adoption, and know that in doing so you may be saving a life. If you can't tell whether the store is selling puppies or is just giving a shelter or rescue group a place to display the animals in their care, think two, three, four, or more times before acquiring a puppy from that store.

Did you already buy a pet-store puppy that likely came from a puppy mill? Don't despair. Housetraining her may be difficult but certainly not impossible. See Chapter 5 for more information.

What is a reputable breeder?

Just what makes a breeder reputable? Here are a few clues to look for:

✔ She's an expert in her breed. I'm not just talking cursory knowledge here; I'm talking someone who knows more about the history of Boxers or the genetic problems of Collies than you could ever imagine. (And if a breeder says her breed doesn't have any such problems, run, don't walk, out her door.)

✔ She raises only a few litters a year. More than that, and you have the makings of a factory breeding operation — in other words, a puppy mill.

✔ She keeps her facilities scrupulously clean. A clean puppy living area ups the odds of dogs and puppies staying healthy — not to mention it encourages the proper development of puppy instincts for a clean den.

✔ She asks you lots of questions. A good breeder cares enough about her puppies to make sure they go to the best possible homes.

✔ She waits until her puppies are 7 to 9 weeks of age before she lets them go to new homes. By that time, the pups have learned some basic canine manners from their mama and have developed enough control to begin housetraining lessons in earnest.

✔ She gives her puppies lots of love and handling and makes sure that they spend time with other people of all ages and both sexes. If a breeder raises her puppies in her family room or kitchen, you're on the right track. If she keeps the pups in an outdoor kennel, walk away.

Animal shelters and rescue groups: Lacking socialization?

Suppose that you've opted for an older dog or a mixed breed from a shelter or rescue group. Will such a dog pose special housetraining challenges? That question has no single answer.

Lots of dogs from animal shelters and rescue groups do just fine with housetraining. In fact, quite a few of them have mastered basic bathroom behavior before you even bring them home. Some, though, may not have done so. And some may be poorly socialized — in other words, they lack the exposure to everyday sights, sounds, and people that enables them to become emotionally well-adjusted animals. This poor socialization may make it tougher for such a dog to become bonded to you and may also make it tougher for you to help him unlearn some bad bathroom habits.

This certainly doesn't mean that the dog you adopt from a shelter or a rescue group can't be housetrained. What may be the case, though, is that the task will be a bit more of a challenge than you expected. You'll get a leg up on that challenge, however, if you find out as much as you can about your dog's background before you bring him home and start teaching him basic bathroom etiquette. Chapter 11 offers more information on how to housetrain the shelter or rescue dog.

Taking the 21st-Century Approach to Housetraining

Today, more people understand that to get what they want from their dogs, they first have to tune in to what their dogs want. People have discovered a lot about how dogs think, feel, and learn. They now know that most dogs don't want to poop or pee anywhere near where they sleep and eat. They understand that every canine likes to have a den to call his own. They realize that dogs don't remember what they've done within a few minutes of having done it. Consistency, patience, and repetition are what you need to teach your dog what you want him to know.

Such knowledge enables you to develop a training approach that helps you help your dog express his instincts in ways that are acceptable to you. In other words, you can train your dog not only to do what you want but to do what *he* wants, too. After you know what your dog can bring to the housetraining process, you have to realize what you need to bring to that same enterprise. This section covers some of the qualities that can help you be the best teacher your dog will ever have.

Seeing your dog's point of view

Any communications theorist, corporate trainer, or psychologist will tell you that to persuade someone to do what you want, you have to put yourself in his shoes. You need to imagine his thoughts and figure out what makes him tick.

Empathy is just as important when you're trying to reach a dog as when you're trying to persuade a person. You need to understand the way your dog views the world and relates to it. In terms of housetraining or any other teaching, you'll be miles ahead of the game if you can think like a dog.

When you think like a dog, you realize that

- Disciplining your dog after she's done something wrong doesn't do any good, because she has no idea what that something-wrong is.

- For many dogs, peeing is much more than an act of elimination — it's a way to communicate with other canines.

- The shy little darling who rolls onto her back and dribbles a bit of urine when you come home hasn't mislaid her bathroom manners. Instead, she's paying homage to you, doggie-style.

- When you're out walking with your four-legged friend at night and she stops suddenly in the middle of the sidewalk, she's not being stubborn; more likely, she sees something that scares her. To you, it's just another garbage can, but to her, it's big and bad and dark and menacing. After you realize what she's feeling and thinking, you can coax her past the object in question instead of yanking on her leash and dragging her to you.

You can't succeed with housetraining — or any type of dog training — by shoving your wishes down your dog's throat and expecting her to swallow them. Force isn't effective; it pits the two of you against each other. Instead, you and your canine companion should be on the same side. You should have a common goal: figuring out how to live happily together.

Being benevolent

A lot of dog-training literature, not to mention amateur trainers or people who think they know the scoop, tell you that dominance and leadership are the keys to training success. "Show your dog who's boss," they say. "Don't let him get away with anything."

Some even recommend that you punish a transgressing dog by grabbing him by the scruff of the neck and rolling him over onto his back *(alpha rolls)* or by hanging him by his collar. Still others advocate that the best way to deal with a fearful dog is to help him face his fear. And many advocate the use of choke chains and prong collars to bring a disobedient dog into line. You won't see any such advocacy here.

At times, a dog owner does need to be a leader. But even at such times, you can be a benevolent leader: the giver of all good things, the source of all things fun, the refuge in times of fear. Such a leader thinks not in terms of dominance and submission but in terms of benevolence and cooperation. You can be your dog's best teacher, but you can also be his best friend — and dominance never needs to be a part of your vocabulary.

Working with your dog's instincts

All my life, I've had curly hair. When I was younger and straight hair was the thing, I plastered all kinds of goop on it, blew and baked it dry and straight, and otherwise just fought Mother Nature. I rarely got the results I wanted — and when I did, Mother Nature invariably found a way to spoil them in the form of rain or simply some high humidity. Then I wised up. I cut my hair super short and let it do its thing. I still use some goop to give it the shine and texture I like, but I don't blow it dry. I wash it, finger-comb it, and go. What, you may ask, does this have to do with housetraining a dog? Everything. Really.

Just as I became a lot happier with my hair after I started working with its natural tendencies, so can you housetrain your puppy or dog faster when you work with hers. Her need for a den, her desire to keep that den clean, and her ability to learn through consistency and repetition can all help her become a housetraining ace much faster than she did back in the day when all Mom had to work with was a rolled-up newspaper and a boatload of totally understandable frustration. You just have to use your dog's instincts to your advantage. But then, that's why you're reading this book.

Creating a schedule

I admit it: About some things in life, dog-related and not, I can be a total fanatic. Creating a schedule for the canine housetrainee is one of those things. Why? Because, quite simply, having a schedule is a great way to reduce the time it takes your dog to get the hang of housetraining. The training process becomes a whole lot easier when you feed your dog, play with him, and let him eliminate at the same times every single day.

A schedule plays right into your dog's need for repetition, consistency, and predictability. A schedule also makes it a whole lot easier for you to anticipate when your dog needs to pee and poop and then to get him to the right place before he has an accident.

There's no one-schedule-fits-all timetable. You need to put together a regimen that fits your dog's age, his degree of housetraining prowess, and the housetraining method you're using. You can find more info on how to create this kind of schedule in Chapters 6 and 7.

Rewarding the good, ignoring the goofs

No, this section isn't an advertorial for the Reverend Norman Vincent Peale's treatise on *The Power of Positive Thinking*. But frankly, he had a point: A whole lot of power lies in positive thinking — and in positive training, too.

Think about that old approach to dog training I talk about at the beginning of this chapter. Basically, it revolves around finding your dog doing something wrong and then punishing him for doing so. But that approach frequently doesn't work very well. All too often, dogs don't know what they're doing wrong, much less how to do something right.

The opposite, positive approach works much better than the negative one. Instead of pouncing on your dog for messing up, look for him to do the right thing — and when he does (trust me, he will), reward him lavishly. That reward can come in the form of verbal praise, loving hugs and petting, tasty treats, or even all three. In any case, take a positive approach, not a negative one. (Wondering what kinds of treats to give your dog? Never fear: Just about everything you ever wanted to know about dog treats appears in Chapter 4.)

Of course, you don't just wait passively for your dog to do the right thing. As part of your approach, you need to actively guide him into performing the maneuvers you want him to perform, using his instincts to help him get the idea a little faster. And when he does get the idea, don't forget to praise him to the skies. You have to reward him for doing what you want him to do.

By consistently showing your dog what you want him to do and then rewarding him for doing so, you're conditioning your dog to do the right thing. You're upping the odds that he'll do what you want him to do every time you want him to do it.

Remember reading about Pavlov's dogs in science class? The Russian scientist actually got the dogs to salivate by giving each dog a food reward — a treat — every time a bell rang. The dogs learned that the ringing bell would precede getting a treat, and they began to look forward to getting that treat. They were primed for that food reward, and as a result, their mouths mouth began to water.

You don't have to wear a white coat and have a fancy laboratory to condition your dog the same way Pavlov conditioned his. Simply show your pooch what you want and immediately reward him for doing what you've shown him — whether it's the first time he pees in your backyard or the hundredth time he anoints a tree instead of the rug in your bedroom. By giving him that reward, you're letting him know that he's done something that pleases you, and you give him an incentive to do that something again.

What if he does something wrong? If he pees on your carpet, you clean it up without any comment. If he poops on your brand-new hardwood floor, you whisk the mess away. Period. You don't yell at him. You don't punish him. You certainly don't rub his nose in it. You just get rid of the mess and move on. (For the lowdown on the fine art of cleaning up the right way, see Chapter 3.)

If you catch your dog in the act of peeing or pooping in the wrong place, view the situation as a teaching opportunity for you and a learning opportunity for him. Interrupt him in the act and take him to the right place: the place where you've decided he should do his bathroom business.

Being consistent

Yes, I know. You've already got so much going on in your oh-so-busy life that you can't possibly remember what color your dog's pee was yesterday or when she last pooped. Believe me, I sympathize. Everyone is on information overload. I, too, have trouble remembering what day it is. Sometimes I even forget that Allie has peed within a minute of her actually doing so.

But take heart. Help for memory-impaired folks is here: consistency. In housetraining terms, *consistency* means having your dog eat, drink, pee, and poop at the same times and places every day. You create a routine that the two of you eventually can do in your sleep (or almost, anyway).

By adopting a consistent routine for your dog's dining and toileting activities, you help not only your own memory but also your dog's ability to housetrain faster. Dogs learn through repetition, so when you and she do the same things at the same times in the same places each day, she'll come to expect that you'll be doing those things.

This consistency affects your dog both physically and mentally. The repetition that you establish in feeding and housetraining your dog conditions her body as well as her mind. After all, you may be physically conditioned to expect that early morning jog or a second cup of coffee at the same time each day — and without the jog or joe, you don't feel quite right. You don't like that feeling, so you stick with your exercise and/or coffee routine; it becomes a habit. By establishing similar routines with your dog, you're helping to make housetraining a habit for her. When her body gets used to the routine you set up for her, she'll be primed to poop and pee when and where you want her to.

Don't worry, though. After your dog is truly housetrained, you don't have to be quite such a fanatic about repetition and consistency. Your dog will have the control she needs to hold it a little longer if your schedule hits an unexpected snag. Still, keeping to at least a semblance of routine is a good idea, even when your four-legged friend is a housetraining ace.

Attending to details

Have you ever toilet-trained a child? If so, you know the importance of paying attention to seemingly trivial details, such as when he last peed in the potty, when he last did a doo-doo in his diaper, or what he ate for dinner the night before he had a funny-colored bowel movement.

The same is true when you're housetraining your dog. During this process, you need to remember what you fed your four-legged friend and when you did so. Recalling how long it's been since he last peed or pooped is always a good idea. And knowing what his pee or poop normally looks like is important so that you can tell when he may be sick. In fact, your dog's pee and poop can tell you a lot about his overall health. (For more information on this topic, see Chapter 10.)

Paying attention to details also means taking the time to observe your dog and discover what makes him the unique individual he is. For example, do you know the answers to these questions?

  ✔ Does he lift his leg when he pees? Does he like to lift both legs (one at a time, of course)? Or does he not bother lifting his leg at all?

✔ Does he need to eliminate right after he eats, or does he like to wait awhile?

✔ Does he like to pee in the same spot all the time, or is he an I'll-do-it-anywhere piddler?

✔ Does he circle and sniff before doing his business? Or does he suddenly stop midstride and do the deed before you quite realize what's happening?

✔ Is he a little introvert who sometimes releases some urine when you greet him? Or is he an extrovert who offers a wagging tail and canine grin to everyone he meets?

Think of the stories you tell your friends about your dog. What are some funny things he's done? How about the sweet things, the poignant things? What are some of his quirks — potty-related and otherwise?

What, you ask, do all these questions have to do with house-training? A lot. The better you know your dog, the more you can empathize with him. The more you can empathize with him — to think the way he does — the better able you are to adjust his housetraining lessons to his unique character and perspective. And the better able you are to fine-tune your housetraining to his character, the more effective your housetraining efforts are overall.

This personalized — or rather, dog-specific — approach is particularly true with respect to your dog's bathroom habits. By paying attention to what he does when he pees or poops, you can better anticipate when he's going to go — and intervene when he's going to go in the wrong place.

Chapter 3

Getting Your Home in Housetraining Order

*B*efore you can start housetraining your puppy or adult dog, not only do you have to get yourself ready — you have to get your home ready. A domicile that's not adjusted to the needs of both the housetrainee (your dog) and the housetrainer (you) can sabotage the efforts of both person and pooch.

Not to worry. In this chapter, I cover everything from finding the right crate to choosing the perfect potty spot —whether you plan to have your canine companion do her pottying indoors or out.

Readying Your Dog's Room: The Crate

Professional dog trainers and experienced dog owners have dealt with a lot of puppy pee and doggie doo. Not surprisingly, they've gotten housetraining down to a science. And just about every one of them will tell you that using a crate makes housetraining easier, quicker, and more effective than any other method.

"A crate?" you ask. "How can that be? They look like cages, not potty-training devices." Looks, however, can be deceiving. I've housetrained dogs with the help of a crate, and I've housetrained dogs without one. I'm a believer: I think crates are unquestionably the way to go if you want your dog to become a housetraining ace as soon as possible.

Understanding why every dog needs (and wants) a crate

Few objects are more important to a wild or domestic canine than the den — that safe, secure place that the animal can call his own. A crate makes a perfect doggie den. It's compact, it's cozy (or you can make it so with some well-chosen crate accessories), and it's dark inside (or you can render it so by draping a towel or blanket atop the crate). And because a crate is open on one side but enclosed on the other three, it offers the dog a safe, secure window through which he can watch his world.

Dogs who are introduced to the crate at a young age soon grow to love their special spaces, and an older dog can learn to at least tolerate a crate when introduced to one properly. Either way, the attachment is well worth cultivating because doing so enables you to tap into a crucial component of your canine companion's denning instinct.

Most domestic dogs do just about anything to avoid peeing or pooping in their dens. When that den is a crate, a dog learns to hold his pee and poop whenever he's inside. If possible, he lets his floodgates open only when he's away from these cherished structures of safety.

Sounds simple, doesn't it? Well, using a crate to potty train your dog is simple, but it's not quite effortless. You can't just run out, buy a crate, and shove your dog into it with the idea that you'll housetrain him at warp speed. Housetraining just doesn't work that way. Housetraining is a fine art, and it starts with figuring out which size and type of crate to buy for your dog.

Finding the right fit: Types of crates

To begin with, you can choose from two basic types of crates: plastic and wire. *Plastic crates,* also known as *carriers,* are molded two-piece units with doors at their fronts and ventilation at their sides. *Wire crates* are made from panels of welded metal wire that are hinged together. Figure 3-1 shows the differences between the two.

This section explains the benefits and drawbacks of these two crate types. Ultimately, which type of crate to use is up to you. Just assess what your future needs are likely to be and make an educated guess as to which type of crate your dog will likely prefer.

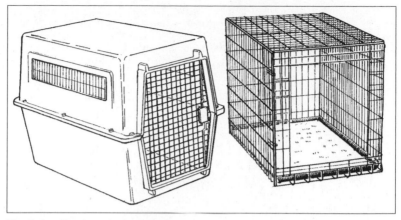

Figure 3-1: Plastic and wire crates.

Plastic crates

Plastic crates offer several advantages over wire ones:

- ✔ Because they're enclosed on three sides (except for the vents), plastic crates can easily become the snug, dark, cozy dens most dogs crave. I chose a plastic crate for my shy Shetland Sheepdog, Cory, because I thought he'd be happier having a dark place in which to hide rather than an open-air abode.

- ✔ Plastic crates generally meet airline specifications for pet shipment as baggage or cargo — an important consideration if you plan to travel by air with your canine companion.

- ✔ Plastic crates often cost a little less than wire crates do.

Plastic crates do have their downsides, though. For example, they can take up more than a little storage space because they don't collapse or fold. In addition, the plastic makes these crates more vulnerable than wire crates to the ravages of canine teeth.

Wire crates

Wire crates also have some advantages:

- ✔ These crates' all-around openness allows your dog to see what's going on when he's lounging in his doggie abode. If your dog doesn't like such openness, you can throw a blanket over the top and sides of the wire crate to create a more enclosed den.

✔ Wire crates are totally collapsible, which means you can stash them away in tiny places when you're not using them.

✔ Wire crates are far easier to adjust for size than plastic crates are. I chose a wire crate for my Golden Retriever puppy, Allie, for just that reason.

✔ Dogs who can't stop chewing don't get anywhere with wire crates — and that's a big advantage in the wire-versus-plastic debate.

✔ Wire crates offer more ventilation than plastic ones do. If your pooch is a snub-nosed breed, such as a Pug or Boston Terrier, opt for a wire crate; such dogs are prone to breathing difficulties.

Like plastic crates, wire crates also carry a couple of disadvantages: They're not considered acceptable for airline travel, and they cost more than their plastic counterparts do.

Adjusting for size

Picking the right size of crate for your dog is crucial — not just for when he's a puppy but also for when he's an adult dog.

A correctly sized crate is just large enough for your dog to comfortably stand up, turn around, and lie down in. A smaller crate will cramp your canine companion. A larger crate will allow your dog to sleep and eat at one end of the crate and relieve himself at the other, which defeats the whole purpose of using the crate.

Either type of crate — wire or plastic — comes in several sizes. For example, one major retailer offers wire crates in four sizes that range from 30 x 20 x 23 inches to 48 x 30 x 35 inches. This retailer also offers a plastic crate in four sizes that range from 28 x 20.5 x 21.5 inches to 40 x 27 x 30 inches.

Does the need to keep the crate the right size mean that you must buy a new one each time your puppy's size increases significantly? Fortunately, the answer is no. You can actually buy one crate that can serve as your dog's den from puppyhood on. The secret: Buy an adult-sized wire crate and block off some of the inside space while your dog is a puppy. Many wire crates come with dividers, wire panels that are similar to the plates at the back of the drawers in metal file cabinets. You simply slide the divider back as your puppy grows and needs a bigger crate. The budget-friendly result is that you have to buy only one crate for your dog's lifetime.

A softer side to crating?

In addition to plastic and wire crates, a third kind of carrier is available: a *soft-sided carrier.* These carriers are lighter and easier to set up than plastic or wire crates, but they're not good for housetraining, especially puppies. The reason: Such crates can't withstand the ravages of canine teeth. Stick with a wire or plastic crate for in-home housetraining.

Investing in crate accessories

For the sake of your dog's comfort and your own convenience, you may want to invest in a few crate accessories:

- ✔ **Mats:** Chief among the crate accessories is some kind of soft mat or carpet for the crate. Crate manufacturers make a variety of mats and carpets to fit their products, including luxurious items such as cut-to-fit mats made of synthetic sheepskin and more basic (but still very comfortable) plastic polyurethane foam mats. Whatever kind of soft flooring you choose, though, make sure that you can clean your dog's crate mat easily — machine-washable is ideal.

  Before you leave your puppy or dog alone in a crate with a mat or cloth, make sure she won't chew or swallow it.

- ✔ **Attachable dishes:** You may want to buy a couple of dishes that you can attach to the inside of the crate door. Some crates come complete with such dishes, but if yours doesn't, pet product manufacturers offer them separately. Such dishes make feeding your dog in her crate much easier — and eating in the crate can help her associate the crate with something positive if she hasn't done so already. Moreover, most airlines require that a crate contain food and water for your jet-setting dog to consume.

- ✔ **Crate dollies:** Traveling canines and their owners may also appreciate having a *crate dolly:* a metal platform with four wheels and a nylon pull handle. Set your dog and her crate atop the dolly, and you can whisk her through the airport with ease.

Situating your doggie's den

The best place to put your dog's crate is wherever you are. Sounds simple enough — until you realize that you don't stay in one place 24/7 or even, sometimes, for more than a few minutes at a time.

Fortunately, you can move a crate just about anywhere. Whenever I'm housetraining a dog, I keep the crate — with the housetrainee inside — in my bedroom with me at night. During the day, I move the crate into the living room near the kitchen so that my dog can see me and the rest of my family moving around the house. When I go downstairs to my office to start writing (I'm fortunate to be able to work from home), both dog and crate come with me.

Keeping your crated canine close not only makes housetraining easier — because you can keep tabs on what your housetrainee is doing — but also helps build the bond between the two of you.

Gearing Up for Outdoor Training

Teaching your pooch to potty outside means that you don't have to provide an indoor doggie bathroom facility; however, you still need some equipment to get the job done. You also need to choose an outdoor potty spot for your dog during the house-training process.

Selecting a potty spot — no matter where you live

Until your dog figures out that the bathroom is outside — and that she can hold her ammo till she gets there — the backyard or some other outdoor area near your house is your best bathroom bet. After all, if you choose a potty spot close to home, you and she won't have to go too far when she needs to poop or pee. After your dog consistently restricts her bathroom maneuvers to the great outdoors — and lasts a couple of hours between potty breaks — you can expand her bathroom horizons beyond your property line.

A young puppy hasn't received all the immunizations she needs to protect her from potentially fatal diseases, such as distemper and canine parvovirus, so the backyard is the best place to start outdoor-training a puppy who's younger than 16 weeks of age. A puppy can catch such diseases through contact with infected dogs' bodily wastes or vomit, so keeping your dog away from these substances is important. Until your pup has completed her shots, keep her potty in your yard and keep her away from areas where other dogs may do their business.

Within your yard, a good potty spot is any place that's fairly close to your house and easy to clean. Plan to clean up your dog's potty area at least once a day.

If you live in an apartment or don't have access to a yard for another reason, you need to walk your puppy to her potty area, but make sure that area isn't where other dogs congregate. Your vet can suggest where to take your apartment-dwelling puppy until she's fully immunized.

Cleaning up after your dog takes on added importance when you start taking her to public places. If your dog poops in a public area, clean it up immediately. Most communities have enacted compulsory cleanup statutes for very good reasons: Dog poop is gross, and it carries disease-bearing organisms.

Securing collars and leashes

Unless you and Fido plan to spend the rest of your lives behind four walls, sooner or later you'll have to venture into the great outdoors. Even if you plan to have your four-legged friend do most of his pottying within your fenced yard, sometimes — such as when you travel — a fenced yard isn't available. Plus, when you get the urge to saunter around your neighborhood on a gorgeous day, won't you want to take Fido with you?

For most pooches and their owners, collars and leashes are facts of life. But these ties don't need to bind you or your dog. This section provides info on choosing the right collar and leash for your four-legged friend.

Types of collars

A collar isn't just a collar. You have lots of doggie neckwear to choose from, and making the right choice is important because if you don't, you run the risk of injuring or even losing your dog. The following list describes the most common safe options for canine necks (and in some cases, bodies):

- ✔ **Leather collars:** These rolled collars resemble leather rings for gigantic fingers and have several advantages, including the fact that they look nice, smell nice (if you like the smell of leather), and don't damage the dog's fur. However, they often cost more than other types of collars and may not provide the control you need if your pooch is an unruly walker. Still, they usually offer good options for puppies, small adult dogs, sensitive pooches, and any adult dog who walks nicely on a leash.

- **Fabric collars:** Collars made from fabric, such as cotton or nylon, resemble very small belts or very large watchbands. Some fabric collars buckle around the dog's neck. You secure others with plastic snap-in clips. Either way, fabric collars are best suited to puppies, small adult dogs, and well-behaved adult canine walkers. These collars generally cost less than leather, but dogs may find them a tad less comfortable because they're wider than leather collars are. They tend to absorb dirt and odor more, too.

- **Head halters:** If your dog is unruly, what can you turn to? One option is the *head halter,* a little nylon device that consists of a loop that goes behind the dog's neck and a second loop that encircles the muzzle. When you place it on the dog, it looks like a horse bridle. The head halter works in the same way a bridle guides a horse — where the head goes, the body follows. Many trainers recommend head halters not only to restrain rambunctious dogs but also to deal with other problems, such as dogs who lunge at other canines and people or who bark a lot while walking. The only disadvantage of the head halter is that some dogs find them itchy and difficult to get used to.

- **No-pull harnesses:** Need another option to keep your pooch from pulling? Try a *no-pull harness,* a device that uses a chest strap to restrain your sled-dog wannabe. By attaching the dog's leash to the chest strap instead of to a collar, you direct pressure to restrain the dog away from the neck and to the chest. No-pull harnesses can be difficult to fit, though — and for the owner of a persistent puller, they may not provide enough control.

- **Body harnesses:** For a small puppy or tiny adult dog, such as a Maltese or a Yorkshire Terrier, a *body harness* may be a much better option than a neck collar. Conventional neck collars may injure a small dog's trachea, but a body harness bypasses that danger because it doesn't touch the dog's neck. Body harnesses are also good options for dogs with back or disk problems or breeds with especially long bodies, such as Dachshunds, because they provide support to the back. Dogs whose heads are smaller than their necks, such as Greyhounds, are also good candidates for body harnesses.

Some collars designed to help owners "correct" their dogs seem more likely to punish than to teach. Practical owners recognize that the following neckwear can hurt or injure their dogs:

- **Slip collars:** Also known as *training collars* or *choke collars,* slip collars were once a mainstay for most dog trainers and owners. The collar's snap-and-release action puts momentary pressure on a dog's neck, which theoretically creates an incentive for the dog to cease her bad behavior.

Measuring up on collar size

To determine your dog's collar size, simply wrap a tape measure fairly loosely around her neck. Add 2 inches to the measurement, and you have her size. For example, a dog whose neck measures 12 inches around needs a 14-inch collar. After you buy the collar and put it on your dog, see whether you can slip two fingers under it. If you can fit only one finger, the collar is too tight; if you can fit more than two, the collar is too loose.

Slip collars can damage a dog's windpipe when used incorrectly — and that happens more often than not, because instead of performing a quick jerk (the correct method), many owners pull on the collar without releasing it. The prolonged pull causes the dog to gasp for breath and often fails to stop the behavior that prompted the owner to pull on the collar in the first place. Bottom line: Dog owners don't need slip collars, because people can use less coercive methods to teach their dogs to walk nicely while on leash.

✔ **Prong collars:** If slip collars are bad, prong collars are worse. This neck gear is exactly what the name says: a collar with prongs that poke the dog's neck when the owner pulls on the leash. Prong collars hurt, and they're cruel. You don't need to inflict pain or be cruel to teach your dog proper walking etiquette, bathroom manners, or anything else. For information on how to teach a dog to walk politely on leash without hurting himself, check out *Dog Training For Dummies*, 2nd Edition, by Jack and Wendy Volhard (Wiley).

Types of leashes

You don't have quite as many leashes to choose from as you do collars. Still, enough variety is out there to stump the average dog owner. As with collars, choosing the right leash is important — for your comfort, your dog's safety, and the safety of other people you and she may encounter while you're exploring the great out-doors. Here's what to consider as you sort through your leashing alternatives:

✔ **Leather leash:** I prefer leather leashes to fabric ones for two reasons: Leather's easier to hold on to, and it lasts a long time. The easier hold comes in handy if your pooch bolts while on the leash, because you can tighten your hold without getting the rope burn on your hand that a cotton or nylon leash can give you. However, leather leashes generally cost significantly more than nylon or cotton leashes of the same length.

✔ **Fabric leash:** Fabric leashes are cheaper, and because they come in lots of colors, they allow you and your dog to make a fashion statement, such as matching the collar color to the leash color. The downsides are that such leashes are generally less durable and less comfortable to grip than their leather counterparts. Some manufacturers have tried to solve the latter problem by adding padding to the handles.

✔ **Retractable leash:** A retractable leash contains a long wire or cord (up to 16 feet) and a hook. The wire resides within a plastic housing, and you can retract the leash by pressing a button or lever on the housing. Retractable leashes can give your dog a feeling of greater freedom, but they also carry several disadvantages. If your dog pulls when she walks, a retractable leash doesn't help you control her; in fact, it may encourage her to pull even harder. These leashes are also tough for other people to see; more than once, I've nearly broken my neck after tripping over such a leash.

At the very least, don't use retractable leashes in populated areas where people can trip over them. Also, don't use them near streets, because your dog can run into the street and become instant roadkill even while attached to the leash.

Leashes can range between 4 feet and 50 feet. For ordinary walks, your best bet is a 6-foot leather or fabric tether. If you opt for a retractable leash, make sure that you don't extend the leash to go beyond 6 feet when you and Fido are in crowds or in public places; in many municipalities, leash lengths longer than 6 feet are illegal.

Containing the situation: Fencing

A fenced yard can provide the foundation for an outdoor paradise for your pooch. It can also make housetraining easier if — and this is a big *if* — you realize that you're still the one who needs to teach Spot when and where to do his business. That means you need to go out with him while he learns to poop and pee outdoors. Only when he's mastered the art of outdoor bathroom behavior can you stay inside while he heads out into the yard to do his thing.

Still, having a fenced yard has several undeniable advantages. For one thing, you don't have to hassle with leashes every time Spot needs to make an outdoor pit stop. And in mornings and evenings, you can stay in your nightwear while you take Spot to his backyard bathroom. That beats having to get dressed and embark on a bleary-eyed walk around the neighborhood with your canine potty trainee.

Just make sure that the fencing you install doesn't awaken the escape artist in your dog's soul. Ask your local hardware store and fencing contract professional which materials are best for keeping canines in the dogs' own yards. And as you or your contractor install the fence, make sure that no openings or crevices — either aboveground or underground — provide portals through which Fido can escape.

Even if you have a fence, don't turn your dog out into the backyard and leave him there all day, every day. Would you want to be in the same place every day, with no way to leave it? All too often, yard dogs become bored dogs — and bored dogs frequently turn into noisy dogs who bark all day or destructive dogs who resort to digging in a desperate attempt to escape the yard or simply amuse themselves. Your neighbors will be grateful if you keep your dog inside with you most of the time. Your yard will look better, too.

Installing a doggie door

A *doggie door,* which is a canine-sized portal built into your door, provides a passage between the inside of your house and your outside yard. Covering the passage is a flap or panel that the dog pushes aside with his nose. Thus, as Figure 3-2 shows, a doggie door enables your dog to take himself outside whenever he needs a potty break.

Figure 3-2: Your canine companion can use a doggie door take himself outside whenever he needs to go.

Zapping electric fencing

Electric fencing sounds like a dream come true. Manufacturers of such invisible boundary systems claim that they teach your dog to stay within the boundaries of your property without your having to erect a conventional fence. The dog wears a special collar that gives him an electrical shock when he crosses the boundaries of your yard.

However, such fencing is far from foolproof. Some determined canines venture beyond their property lines despite getting shocked by their collars, only to refuse to come back home because they don't want to endure another shock upon reentry. Another problem with electric fencing is that other dogs, animals, or people can enter the yard freely, and your dog can't escape from them, which makes him vulnerable.

As with so many other products, electric fencing seems to promise a shortcut to teaching and taking care of your dog. All too often, though, such shortcuts only shorten the path to problems.

A doggie door can be a simple portal-and-flap affair or an elaborate electronic system. Different models can go into walls, French doors, or regular doors. A doggie door can be a godsend for you and your already-housetrained dog: She doesn't have to hold it all day while you're at work, and you don't have to get up to let Bowser out in the middle of the night.

 Make sure that the doggie door leads your dog to a secured area — either a fenced backyard or some sort of dog run. Experts suggest that you close and lock the doggie door when you don't need it (such as when you're home and are able to let the dog outside yourself when he needs to go) and that you install it in an inconspicuous area of your house. These precautions give you the convenience of a doggie door without extending an invitation to burglars or other intruders.

 Don't rely on a doggie door until your pooch has mastered his housetraining fundamentals. For some dogs, figuring out where and when to do their business is complicated enough without also having to learn to maneuver that doggie door flap.

Prepping for Indoor Training

If you choose to have your pooch do the doo inside your home, you don't need to think about fencing or doggie doors at all, and you need to think about leashing your dog only when you go out for a casual stroll. But indoor training still requires some equipment and forethought. In this section, I offer ideas about how to choose the proper receptacles and where to put them inside your house.

Exploring types of indoor potties

Many options are available to the pooch who potties indoors. Those options include the following:

- **Newspapers:** They're cheap, but they're not necessarily neat. The first time you clean up a few squares of newspaper soaked in dog pee, the potential messiness of this enterprise becomes evident. If you don't pick up the paper carefully, the pee that was on the paper may drip down to the floor — or worse, onto you. Plus, those newspapers never look very nice when they're spread out on your floor, even before your dog uses them.

- **Puppy training pads:** Some stores sell absorbent pads you can lay out on the floor, but I don't recommend them. They're messy, and the dog can shred them. Reusing old newspapers is cheaper and more environmentally friendly, too.

- **Litter boxes:** They look better on the floor than newspapers do, and cleanup's a lot more sanitary: Just scoop the used litter into the trash and flush any solid waste down the toilet. But litter boxes aren't as portable or convenient as newspapers, and they're also more expensive.

- **Novelty potties:** Innovative companies are creating indoor potty options for dogs all the time. For example, one novel facility is the UGoDog (www.ugodog.net), which consists of a plastic tray and a plastic grate that lies atop the tray. The dog steps onto the grate and does his business, which drops from the grate into the tray.

I say more about indoor potties in Chapter 7. Ultimately, the indoor potty you choose is a matter of personal preference. If you hate the look of newspapers all over your floor, a litter box or novelty potty may be a good alternative. But if you want to housetrain your pooch as cheaply as possible, newspapers have the edge.

Setting up your dog's indoor living area and potty spot

Indoor training is a lot easier for both people and pooches when the dog's living area — his home within your home — is arranged appropriately. And I say "home within your home" for a very important reason: Until you've fully housetrained your dog, he shouldn't have access to your entire home unless you can be right there to watch his every move.

This no-total-access rule is crucial whether you live in a pocket-sized apartment or an abode that rivals Hearst Castle. That's because if you're not watching what Fido is doing, you're not likely to see when Fido's about to have an accident. Whenever you have to clean up the accident after the fact, you've missed a golden opportunity to remind Fido where he's supposed to do his business.

So during those times you can't pay close attention to your indoor trainee, confine him to a dog-proofed living area that he can call his own. The living area should include the following:

- ✔ A soft, comfy bed, possibly within a crate (see the earlier section "Readying Your Dog's Room: The Crate" for info on choosing the right crate for your dog)
- ✔ A place to eat
- ✔ A place to potty
- ✔ Containment to keep your pooch from making unauthorized forays outside his living area

The containment can take the form of baby gates or an exercise pen, also known as an *x-pen*. An *x*-pen looks like a six-or eight-sided wire crate without a top or bottom. Make sure the gate or *x*-pen is high enough that your puppy can't leap over it, and make sure it touches the floor so he can't squeeze under it.

When you have those essentials, you need to decide where to put them. Here are some factors to consider when figuring out where you should set up your dog's living area:

- ✔ **Your dog's needs:** Your indoor trainee needs more than just a place to sleep, eat, poop, and pee. He also needs to be in the middle of his household's action. A dog is a social being; the closer he is to his people, the happier he is. Plus, the time your puppy or dog spends in the hub of the household gives him the mental and social stimulation he needs to become an easy-to-live-with member of your family.

- ✔ **Your needs:** When figuring out where to place a dog's living area, one of the most important considerations is whether the area is easy to clean. That's because no matter how carefully you follow the instructions in this book, your pooch will have some accidents before he masters the art of proper potty behavior. Removing those accidents easily and thoroughly is crucial — both for your peace of mind and for your four-legged friend's housetraining progress. For those reasons, locating the dog's living area in an uncarpeted room is often a good idea.

✔ **Your home layout:** The place in which you establish your dog's living space needs to have enough room for both you and him to go about the business of living. This consideration may prompt you to place your dog's living area in a different part of your home than someone else would, which is okay. There's no one-size-fits-all best place to locate your puppy's palace.

Many people opt to house their dogs in their kitchens, which often makes sense. After all, kitchens are usually relatively large, the floors are easy to clean, and families tend to gather there more than in any other room in the house. However, corralling a dog in the kitchen may not be practical if that room is very small, as is often the case in many city apartments.

If you have a small kitchen, house your dog in your bedroom with you. By keeping the dog's living area in your bedroom, your dog can spend lots of time with you without your having to watch him every second.

After you decide which room your puppy can share with you, you have to arrange his things. Generally, you need to remember only one cardinal rule here: Place the bed and dishes *away* from the designated potty area. By doing so, you encourage your dog's instinctive desire to keep his sleeping and dining areas clean.

When your dog is first learning to potty properly, cover all but a small strip of the entire living area with newspaper. Then, as he begins to show that he knows where to go, gradually reduce the papered-over area. You can also put some plastic, such as a shower curtain, between the papers and the floor to keep your dog's pee from soaking through the papers.

Doing the Dirty Work: Cleanup Equipment

Countless communities have jumped onto the canine cleanup bandwagon. From New York to San Francisco, American cities and towns have enacted laws that require their citizens to clean up immediately after their dogs poop. Failure to do so can lead to hefty fines for the human offenders.

The cities with pooper-scooper laws aren't just concerned with the gross-out factor of pet poop. Animal waste from yards or near streets often slips into storm drains and streams. The extra fertilizer encourages algae to grow and carries poop-dwelling parasites to your favorite fishing spots and swimming holes. Yuck.

In this section, you explore the best ways to clean up after your four-legged friend.

Choosing an outdoor cleanup method

Cleaning up outside isn't just a matter of aesthetics; it's a matter of sanitation. What's the best way to clean up your dog's poop when she goes outside? Here are a few methods to choose from, along with tips on how to properly execute them.

Bagging it

The quickest, easiest way to get rid of a dog's poop is to put it in a plastic bag and then either drop the bag in a trash can or flush the bag's contents down a toilet.

You may think that this method has a high gross-out factor — and it can. But it doesn't have to. Here are the two keys to effective bagging: using the right size of bag and developing the proper bagging technique.

 Choose a bag that's large enough to hold your dog's poop, such as an empty bread bag or the plastic bag that your newspaper came in. Both of these types are oblong, which greatly eases your ability to get the poop into the bag instead of on yourself. You may want to carry two bags at a time — some dogs poop more than once during bathroom breaks.

 Before you use your bag, make sure that it doesn't have any holes, especially at the bottom. Picking up a bunch of dog doo only to have it hit the ground again is a surefire recipe for frustration.

After you have the right bag, gathering up the poop is easy. Here's how:

1. **Pull the plastic bag over one hand like a glove.**

   If you're cleaning up while walking your dog, loop the leash around your wrist and pull the bag over the leashed hand.

2. **Pick up the poop with your bagged hand.**

3. **With your other hand, grasp the open end of the bag and pull the bag inside out.**

   The poop will now be inside the bag.

4. **Knot the bag and drop it into the nearest trash can, or take the bag inside and flush the contents down the toilet.**

Of course, if you're walking your dog and can't find a trash can nearby, you have to carry the bagged poop until you find one. But take heart. Soon, not even the thought of having to tote your dog's poop around town will gross you out — it'll just be a fact of life.

Scooping it

If you can't bear handling your dog's poop, consider using a pooper-scooper. A *pooper-scooper* is a long-handled rake, shovel, or spadelike device that enables the owner to scoop up the poop without having to bend down and get close to it.

Digesting it

If you don't want to put your dog's poop in the trash, or if you like the idea of high-tech waste disposal, you may want to acquire a waste digester system. This small in-ground system works the same way a septic system does: It liquefies any dog poop deposited there and drains the liquid into the surrounding soil.

The basic waste digester system has two parts: the digester unit itself (including the lid) and the digester mix. Follow these steps to use this system:

1. **Find a convenient but out-of-the-way spot in your yard to install the digester.**

   Don't install a waste digester near a storm drain, water well, or vegetable garden.

2. **Dig a hole about 48 inches deep.**

3. **Install the digester and lid in the hole.**

   The lid should be just a little bit above the ground.

4. **When your dog poops, bring the poop to the digester, remove the lid, and place the poop inside.**

5. **Add some digester mix and some water and replace the lid.**

   Then the digester does its thing.

Help! My lawn is dying!

Plastic bags, pooper-scoopers, and dog-doo digesters do a great job of removing poop from sidewalks and lawns, but they're totally ineffective in dealing with the damage a dog's urine can do to a carpet of green grass. Female dogs are especially lethal to grass, because they squat and urinate in one place. Males, on the other hand, often lift their legs and anoint vertical surfaces such as bushes, trees, and shrubs.

Of course, keeping your dog off the grass does the most to preserve the lush green carpet better known as your front lawn. But if that's not an option — or if your dog gets away from you and takes a whiz on your prized turf — you can try the following options:

✔ **Flush the area.** Immediately after your dog does her duty, saturate the area with water. Doing so dilutes the nitrogen in the urine and reduces the damage the urine causes.

✔ **Change the grass.** Some varieties of grass, such as ryegrass and fescue, are more resistant to urine damage than others. Planting such varieties, at least in the spots that your dog most often anoints, can help save your lawn.

✔ **Give your dog more water.** Giving your dog more water can help dilute her urine before it hits the grass, thereby reducing the damage the urine inflicts.

Digesters are a good option for the same people who go for pooper-scoopers — owners whose dogs do most of their pooping in their own yards. In fact, owners often use the two methods together. They use the scooper to transport the poop to the digester and then use the digester to process the poop.

You can find digesters at pet stores, in pet supply catalogs, and on pet retail Web sites. The cost, including both the digester unit and the digester mix, ranges between $40 and $55. Make sure, though, that your land is suitable for digesters: Soils with heavy clay, land with high water tables, and areas with low temperatures may not be suited for these products. And check your local laws to make sure that digesters are okay for use in your community.

Digesting isn't the same as composting. Composting is a great way to recycle certain materials, but your dog's poop shouldn't be among them. The temperatures in the compost pile don't rise high enough to kill the pathogens in that poop. For safety's sake, dispose of your dog's solid deposit in another way.

Indoor cleaners

Until you fully housetrain your dog — and perhaps even thereafter, if she becomes ill — she's going to make some mistakes. Instead of doing her business outside, on the papers, or in the litter pan, she'll do it inside — on the floor, on the carpet, on the furniture, or even on your bed.

In any case, you want to get rid of the mess as soon as possible. Of course, you want to preserve the surface on which your dog has put her unwelcome deposit, but you need to get rid of the puddle or pile right away for another more important reason: Canine pee or poop is like a magnet to dogs. If Lassie urinates on the carpet and you don't clean up that urine promptly and thoroughly, Lassie will come back to that spot again and again to pee on it.

To prevent repeated accidents, you need to remove not only the pee or poop and the stain it leaves but also any odor it emits. Certain cleaners accomplish all these objectives. Others don't quite do the job.

If you're looking for a product that cleans up your dog's bathroom boo-boos, make sure the product's label specifically states that purpose. Such products contain special enzymes or other properties that break down the dog's waste and neutralize its odor. When the odor is gone, the dog can't smell where she performed her last unauthorized download and, lucky for you, doesn't have any incentive to repeat that performance.

Here are some cleaning products to avoid:

- ✔ **Ammonia:** If you use an ammonia-based cleaner to mop up your dog's accident, you may as well ask her to return to perform an encore. Ammonia smells like urine to dogs, so the odor from an ammonia-based cleaner draws your pooch back to where she peed before and prompts her to do it again.

- ✔ **Club soda:** Some dog owners advocate using club soda in a pinch to clean up a dog's bathroom boo-boo. Although club soda is cheaper and more readily available than a commercial pet stain remover, the soda is much less effective than the commercial product. Club soda may help remove the stain caused by a dog's bathroom accident, but it does nothing to remove the odor.

Other cleaning aids

The products I describe in the preceding sections more than do the job of cleaning up your dog's bathroom byproducts both indoors and out. However, you may want to consider a few other products and services:

- **A black light:** If you think you've removed all traces of stain and odor from your favorite area rug but Fido's still peeing on it, invest $20 or so on a black light. This handy device illuminates old urine stains that you may not be able to see. Use your indoor pet stain cleaner to remove such stains once and for all — and remember that one application may not be enough to do the job.

- **A pooper-scooper service:** Does the very thought of dealing with your dog's poop give you the willies? Do you have mobility problems? Or do you just not have the time to deal with cleaning up your poop-laden yard? If you answered yes to any of these questions, consider hiring a professional poop-scooping company. To find one, type "pooper scooper service" and the state you live in into an Internet search engine. Depending on how populated your state is, you should come up with at least a few hits. Another option: Visit Poop Butler at www.poopbutler.com and check out their Pooper Scooper Directory.

- **Undergarments:** Sometimes even the most trustworthy dog has a health problem that temporarily makes holding water impossible for her to do. Until you and your veterinarian figure out why she's having such problems, you can protect your carpets and furniture by fitting your pooch with an undergarment, such as a doggie diaper, underpants, or even the canine equivalent of a sanitary napkin. Check out Chapter 9 for more info on these garments, and see Chapter 10 for more on illnesses that can cause bathroom problems.

Chapter 4

Feeding Fido: What Goes In Must Come Out

You can't discuss the art of housetraining a dog — much less practice that art successfully — without also discussing what you're going to feed that dog.

The reason is simple: What comes out of your dog in the form of pee or poop is directly related to what you put into him. Consequently, if you control what you feed your four-legged friend, you also exert some control over his bathroom behavior. In this chapter, I explain how that relationship works — and how to take advantage of that relationship as you teach your canine companion proper potty deportment.

Knowing How Feeding and Watering Affect Housetraining

That what-goes-in-eventually-comes-out principle of housetraining manifests itself in countless ways. Here are just a few examples:

> ✔ **What you feed:** This affects the size and consistency of your dog's poop, as well as how often he may need to do the doo. For example, if your dog eats a lot of vegetables, he'll probably need to poop more often than the pooch who prefers more basic canine fare. Vegetables contain relatively high amounts of fiber, and fiber acts as a laxative.

Also, food that's high in salt is likely to make your dog thirsty. Ingesting goodies that have a lot of salt in them, such as many table scraps, may send your pooch to his water dish more often. And the more times your dog tanks up, the more often he's going to need to empty his tank (his bladder).

Even different types of dog food affect your dog's bathroom output. A dog who eats a raw food diet tends to have firmer, more compact stools than a pooch whose diet consists of other fare.

✔ **When you feed:** Timing directly affects when your dog needs to potty. A canine housetrainee who eats his dinner at 5 p.m. needs a post-dinner pit stop earlier in the evening than the dog who sups at 7 p.m.

Experts explain that the very act of eating can activate a dog's *gastrocolic reflex:* In layman's terms, that means the act of chowing down triggers your dog's urge to go.

✔ **How you feed:** A pooch who has to gulp his food amid a chaotic atmosphere may suffer from an upset stomach — which in turn can result in more frequent, looser, and tougher-to-clean-up bowel movements.

Understanding Nutrients: What Dogs Need to Eat

Just like you, dogs need certain basic nutrients to survive, much less thrive. Those nutrients include proteins, fats, vitamins, and minerals. This section explains why they're necessary and how your dog can obtain them.

Much more info about dog food and nutrition is in *Dog Health and Nutrition For Dummies,* by M. Christine Zink (Wiley). For up-to-date information, consider subscribing to the *Whole Dog Journal* (www. whole-dog-journal.com), which ranks commercial foods every year and accepts no advertising.

Proteins

Proteins enable the body to convert food into energy. They also promote healthy growth and cell repair and affect both metabolism and nervous system function. Commercial dog foods contain several types of protein:

  ✔ **Meat protein:** From animal organs or muscles

  ✔ **Animal protein:** From any other part of the animal that contains protein, such as hooves and hair

  ✔ **Grain protein:** From exactly where the name says it's from

Not all proteins are created equal. A dog can digest meat or animal proteins more easily than she can digest grain proteins. The more digestible the protein, the better it is for the dog.

One clear indicator of dog food's digestibility is the size of the dog's stools. Small stools mean more food has been digested, and larger stools (from the same size of dog) indicate that less food has been digested. Consequently, a dog who eats food that's high in meat-based protein will probably have smaller, more compact poop than the dog of the same size whose food is composed of more grain.

Proteins are made up of amino acids, ten of which a dog has to get through diet. If proteins don't contain all ten *essential amino acids,* those proteins are considered incomplete.

Meat protein sources are more likely to be complete, so at the very least, you should choose high-quality foods that are lower in grain-based proteins and higher in meat-based proteins. The list of ingredients on a dog food package label shows which ingredients predominate and the percentage of each ingredient in the food.

The amount of protein a dog needs varies throughout a dog's life. For example, puppies need more protein than adult dogs do, because puppies are still growing and need extra energy. Protein requirements also vary between dogs with different activity levels. A Border Collie who spends her days herding livestock needs more protein in her diet than a Bulldog whose fastest pace is likely to be a leisurely amble.

Fats

Fats are essential to maintaining healthy hair and skin. They also help keep a dog's body temperature stable and promote healthy digestion. And because they contain more calories than protein, fats are sources of energy. Of course, too much fat in a diet — particularly when coupled with a lack of exercise — leads to extra poundage on both pooches and people. Fats are in many foods and in supplements such as fatty acid capsules.

What dogs may not need: Carbohydrates

In discussing dogs' dietary needs, I don't mention an element that's common in doggie diets: carbohydrates. I have a reason for that: It's not at all clear that dogs need them — and in fact, at least some dogs are better off without them.

Carbs are just another source of energy. Plants use light to create carbohydrates from carbon dioxide and water. Most carbs in dog foods come from grains such as corn and wheat. They may also come from legumes, particularly soybeans. But those grains can cause problems for some dogs in the form of food allergies and learning problems, and they may cause others to put on too much weight.

For those reasons, bagging carbs completely in favor of diets based solely on meats, veggies, and fruits may be an option worth considering. For more information, talk to your vet.

Vitamins and minerals

Vitamins and minerals enable the body to properly process proteins and fats (as well as carbohydrates; see the nearby sidebar for more on this topic). They also help sustain a dog's immune system, maintain coat quality, and prevent disorders ranging from bone problems to behavioral difficulties.

Vitamins and minerals may be incorporated into a commercial food or dispensed as a supplement in the form of pills or caplets. To be fully effective, vitamins and minerals must be balanced properly. For example, calcium supplements aren't fully effective unless they're combined with magnesium.

Determining the Diet That's Best for Your Dog

Your dog food choices depend mainly on your dog: her preferences, her age, and her lifestyle. For example, you may go for a higher protein food if your canine companion is a growing puppy and/or is very active. Foods that are lower in protein content may be better for adult dogs, particularly if they spend most of their time being couch potatoes. And if your dog doesn't like the brand you're currently feeding her, trying another makes sense. No food, no matter how nutritious it is, will do your dog much good if she refuses to eat it.

The fact that your dog likes her food isn't enough. It also needs to be good for her. Here are some questions to ask to help you evaluate whether the food your pooch likes is good for her, too:

- ✔ **Is her poop firm and compact, or is it loose, bulky, and stinky?** If the latter is the case, your four-legged friend may be having trouble digesting the food. Consider switching to a higher quality food: one that lists a meat protein as the first ingredient and has a lower grain content, if any.

- ✔ **Is her skin dry and flaky?** If so, her food may lack fatty acids. Consider switching to a food that has a higher fat content or consulting your vet about getting a fatty acid supplement.

- ✔ **Is your home-alone dog acting jittery? Does she seem spazzed?** The protein content in her food may be too high. Consider switching her to a lower-protein product.

- ✔ **Is your pooch porking out?** Look for a higher protein, lower fat food. Pudgy pups (and adult dogs) are at greater risk for developing health problems than their slimmer canine brethren are.

Make sure that any switches from one dog food to another are very gradual. A dog who's switched suddenly from one food to another is very likely to acquire an upset stomach. As you experiment to find a dog food that your canine companion likes, switch foods gradually. Prevent upsets by mixing progressively larger amounts of the new food with the old over a period of several days.

In the following subsections, I discuss some of your feeding choices, including commercial, home-cooked, and raw foods.

Considering commercial dog foods

Years ago, dogs ate whatever people didn't feel like eating: table scraps, unwanted leftovers, and stuff otherwise destined for the garbage can. Many dogs also procured their own protein sources by killing animals such as barnyard rodents or rabbits who strayed into the fields where the dogs liked to roam. But just as life on the farm became a thing of the past for many people and their pooches, interest in breeding prize-winning dogs burgeoned. So at the same time that dogs could no longer scrounge up their own grub, their increasingly busy owners began demanding better fare than those table scraps, leftovers, and killed vermin for their canine companions.

Enter the livestock feed industry, which began to expand its market beyond cattle, hog, and poultry producers to also include dog owners. The industry developed different combinations of grains and meat products into dog foods that were convenient to buy and easy to prepare. As time passed and nutritional knowledge accumulated, the quality of some manufactured foods improved. This section discusses dry and canned commercial foods as well as some special diets.

Forms of commercial dog food

Today's dog owner has a huge variety of commercial foods from which to choose for her dog, but commercial dog foods are generally dry or canned. Table 4-1 shows how they compare.

Table 4-1	Comparing Dry and Canned Food	
Category	**Dry Food (Kibble)**	**Canned Food**
Spoilage time	Can last for weeks if kept in an airtight container	After you open the can, you have to keep it in the fridge and use it up within 7 days
Dental effects	Can keep your dog's teeth clean	May cling to teeth
Nutritional value	If properly formulated, can be a viable option; sometimes contains too many carbs and not nearly enough proteins from meat	More likely to have higher content from meat and less from grain
Cost	Relatively inexpensive	More expensive because of shipping costs
Dog enjoyment	Dogs don't always enjoy total kibble diets and may find such regimens too dull	The moisture and aroma are generally more pleasing to pooch palates than dry food
Effects on poop	Poop is compact, dry, and easy to clean up	Poop is bigger and wetter than that of dogs who stick to kibble

Pet food manufacturers have also come up with all kinds of other options for feeding your four-legged friends, including freeze-dried foods; semi-moist foods that come in tubes (and make great treats); and base-type foods that, when mixed with meat, provide a complete meal.

Specially formulated diets

Although the same types of ingredients appear in virtually every commercial dog food, the amounts of each vary. Many of these variances are deliberate. Pet food manufacturers combine these ingredients in different ways to create foods designed to address a wide range of conditions and life stages. These special diets include the following:

- **Life cycle diets:** These dog foods are based on the premise that a dog's age affects what her nutritional requirements are. Life cycle diets often include food for young puppies, older puppies, adult dogs, and senior dogs. They've been a staple of the industry for many years.

- **Activity diets:** More recently, manufacturers have developed higher-protein pet foods designed for certain high-energy canine activities. The canine candidates for these specialized foods include dogs who are extremely active, dogs who are involved in performance activities such as showing and agility, and female dogs who are pregnant or nursing puppies.

- **Condition diets:** Several pet food companies have developed a wide range of dog foods designed to aid in the treatment of a dizzying array of conditions. For example, one company has developed a food that's been proven to help extend the lives of dogs who have cancer, and other companies are finding that high-carbohydrate, lower-protein diets may be a potent weapon in combating these dreaded diseases.

  Meanwhile, several companies have developed product lines that aim to help pooches with food allergies. Such diets frequently eliminate corn, soybeans, or wheat from their foods, because some dogs are allergic to these ingredients. These foods may substitute lamb or chicken or really exotic proteins (would you believe bison or kangaroo?) for beef and also include novel carbohydrates such as potatoes or yams.

  Other diets aim to aid in the treatment of conditions that range from accident recovery to weight management.

Making home-prepped dog foods

Giving your dog home-prepped foods may take more work, but you have more control over what goes into your dog's diet. In this section, I discuss cooking meals for your dog and following the BARF diet, which is the cornerstone of the raw-foods movement.

Fixing your dog home-cooked meals

Sooner or later, no matter how committed you are to giving your dog commercial food, you're probably going to have to fix a doggie dinner yourself. A common reason to give your dog a homemade meal is that your four-legged friend has a bout of diarrhea (and diarrhea is pretty common among dogs, so this possibility is more than likely). Among the remedies your veterinarian probably will suggest is to put your dog on a bland diet. This regimen consists of gentle, easy-to-digest foods, such as ground beef and rice, that are guaranteed to soothe your pooch's tender tummy and put him well along on the road to recovery.

Owners can go further than just creating bland diets when a dog feels unwell. You may want to give your pooch home-cooked fare for a larger portion of his total food intake. Start with these titles: *The Natural Pet Food Cookbook: Healthful Recipes for Dogs and Cats,* by Wendy Nan Rees and Kevin Schlanger (Wiley), and *Holistic Guide for a Healthy Dog,* by Wendy Volhard and Kerry Brown, DVM (Wiley).

Going raw with the BARF diet

If you decide to find out more about canine feeding options, you'll probably come across the BARF diet. Rest assured that this food plan won't induce bulimia in your dog or anyone else. BARF is an acronym for *biologically appropriate raw food,* and it's just what it sounds like: a food plan in which you feed raw bones, raw meat, and fresh vegetables to your canine companion.

Dog owners who favor going raw contend the following:

- A doggie menu based entirely on uncooked meats, vegetables, and bones most closely approximates what wild animals eat. Such a diet may allow dogs to live longer, healthier lives.

- Dogs who eat raw food have cleaner teeth and glossier coats.

- The BARF diet can bring an end to food allergies and ear infections. (My own dog has enjoyed a near-total absence of ear infections since I began to BARF her four years ago.)

- Dogs who've gone raw produce stools that are smaller, firmer, and easier to pick up than is the case with dogs fed with conventional fare — a great benefit when you're housetraining!

Many breeders, dog show enthusiasts, and owners of performance dogs enthusiastically endorse the BARF diet, as do many veterinarians who practice alternative veterinary medicine.

Giving dogs dietary supplements

You may take a multivitamin every day. If such supplements help you, wouldn't your dog benefit from the same? Well, maybe. The answer depends on your dog and how you choose to feed her. For example, if you fix your dog's food yourself, you may need to add supplements such as extra vitamins or fatty acids to ensure that she gets the proper balance of nutrients. On the other hand, devotees of commercial food may not need to add anything to the food at all.

However, even canine consumers of commercial food need some supplements if they've been dealing with certain health conditions. For example, your vet may prescribe fatty acid supplements if your dog's coat and skin are excessively dry.

The bottom line on the supplements question is that the answer depends on your individual dog. Consider her needs carefully — preferably with the help of your veterinarian.

More-traditional vets, along with pet food manufacturers, don't agree with BARF enthusiasts. They worry that raw bones can cause internal injuries or choking and note that any use of raw food ups the odds of contracting *Salmonella* or other bacterial poisoning — either by the dog or by the person handling the food. Others have found that some dogs who eat raw food develop chronic diarrhea or vomiting.

One formerly formidable argument against the BARF diet — that it's time-consuming and inconvenient to prepare — has pretty much evaporated. That's because several companies now prepare and sell raw food for dogs and cats. Among these companies are Aunt Jeni's Home Made (www.auntjeni.com), Bravo! (www.bravorawdiet.com), and Oma's Pride (www.omaspride.com). These products are hitting more and more pet food specialty stores, but if your local outlet doesn't carry them, check the companies' Web sites to find distributors; I purchase my Allie's raw food through a cooperative that's run by a local dog trainer who doubles as a distributor. Failing that, you may be able to get the products of your choice shipped directly to your door.

Feeding a raw diet is not for every dog or for every owner. If the idea of handling raw food makes your stomach queasy, bag the idea of BARFing and don't feel guilty about it. And if your dog has a compromised immune system or a lot of chronic illnesses, a BARF diet probably is not a good choice.

Before you make your decision about BARFing your dog, consult some expert sources. A fine book to start with is *The Holistic Dog Book: Canine Care for the 21st Century,* by Denise Flaim (Howell Book House).

Doggie dining preferences

My late Sheltie, Cory, made it clear to my family that he didn't like to eat by himself. He was a semi-social diner; he liked knowing that I was nearby while he ate his breakfast or dinner in the family kitchen. If I left any of the rooms that adjoin the kitchen, he'd stop eating and come look for me. To ease his apparent worries, I learned to stick around while Cory ate. By contrast, my current canine companion, Allie, doesn't care whether I'm around or not, as long as the food is there. She comes looking for me after her meal so she can get her after-meal chewie.

Cory also seemed to prefer that his dining experiences not be overly stimulating. Any household activity that diverted or excited him, such as taking the trash outside (he apparently believed it was his job to escort the trash-taker to the front door), would prompt him to stop eating — at least until the excitement abated.

My husband, daughter, and I learned to cater to Cory's dining whims. That seemed only fair. After all, we made it clear that we expected him to respect *our* dining preferences. For example, we taught him that it's not nice to stare at human diners, no matter how much he may have wanted one of those diners to drop him a morsel or two.

Serving Your Dog

The way you serve your dog can affect his digestion (and thus, what he produces) almost as much as what you serve him does. This section covers the where, when, and how of feeding your dog, plus it includes some dishing about dishes.

Picking the place to feed your dog

Choosing where to feed your dog depends mostly on what works for you. The most convenient canine dining room is one that's located close to where you prepare meals, if not actually in the same place. In most households, that place is the kitchen, which has a couple of advantages:

- ✔ For you, the big plus is that the kitchen is usually the room that's easiest to clean: a big consideration if, like many dogs, your four-legged friend doesn't eat all that neatly.

- ✔ For your dog, the big plus to kitchen dining is that the rest of the household usually congregates there. That means a lot to a social animal like your canine companion, who's happiest when she's hanging out with the other members of her pack.

Dogs don't like eating anywhere near their bathrooms. If you're training your dog to potty indoors, don't feed her in the same place she does her business. Place her dishes at least a few feet away from the indoor potty.

You can also feed your dog in her crate — in fact, doing so can help your dog learn her basic bathroom manners more quickly. That's because crate-based dining gives your four-legged friend another reason to like this makeshift doggie den. In addition, eating in the crate helps a pooch learn to refrain from pooping or peeing as soon she's finished a meal. The reason, of course, is that she doesn't want to soil her den. Many plastic crates include small dishes that you can attach to the inside doors.

Setting the canine dining ambience

What sort of dining atmosphere do you prefer? Do you like a noisy, hectic, Grand-Central-Station eating experience? Or do you prefer a quieter, more low-key dining environment? Do you like eating with a crowd? With one or two other people? Alone? Of course, those questions don't have any one correct answer. Every response simply reflects the responder's personal preference. And that's exactly the point. You may have definite ideas about the ideal dining experience — and your dog may, too (see the nearby sidebar "Doggie dining preferences" for some examples).

Although dogs may have individual ideas about how they like to dine, a few canine dining concepts apply to all pooches. Here are some ideas on how to make mealtime a good time for any dog:

- **Minimize stress.** Dogs who are stressed out while eating are more likely to have upset stomachs than those whose meal-times are relatively tranquil. A pooch with a troubled tummy may get gassy or even vomit after his meal.

- **Separate siblings.** If yours is a multi-dog household, feed each canine pack member separately — in different locations and/ or at different times. That way, neither dog will feel the need to scarf down his food in order to keep the other pooch from grabbing his grub.

- **Let him linger — a little.** Your dog deserves a chance to savor his breakfast, lunch, or dinner. Give him at least 15 minutes to finish his meal. However, giving your dog an unlimited amount of time to eat is not a good idea. Doing so can wreak havoc with potty routines and thus defeat the purpose of setting up a feeding schedule. If your dog hasn't finished his meal in 30 minutes, toss it.

✔ **Wash those dishes.** No one, including your dog, likes to eat fresh food off dirty dishes. Be sure to wash your dog's food dishes after every meal, either by hand or in the dishwasher. Water dishes need daily washing, too.

I truly believe that decoding a dog's dining desires can make for better bathroom behavior. A dog who's happy with his dining environment will eat more regularly — and a dog who eats more regularly will probably eliminate more regularly than a dog who's too distracted to attend to what's in her dish. Any way you look at it, what goes in eventually comes out — but what *doesn't* go in ultimately goes nowhere except to the garbage disposal.

Selecting your dog's dinnerware

No discussion of how to feed a dog is complete without a little dishing about dishes. They come in a wide range of sizes and shapes. Your best bet is to choose the one that best fits your dog's size, age, and appetite:

✔ A short-faced breed, like a Pug, does well with a wide, shallow bowl.

✔ A long-eared dog, such as a Cocker Spaniel, fares better with a narrow, deep bowl.

✔ Puppies may find eating easier with a flying saucer–shaped bowl that has a raised center; such a bowl keeps food where they can reach it. That kind of bowl can also help dogs who otherwise tend to inhale their food to slow down and really enjoy it.

Next, consider the material. Experts give a unanimous thumbs-up to stainless steel dishes because they're easy to clean and can't be demolished by a teething puppy.

Ceramic dishes are easy to clean and impervious to chewing. They also have the added advantage of weight, which keeps them from being knocked over.

Imported ceramic bowls — especially those that come from Central America — may contain lead, which can be toxic to dogs as well as to people. A prudent owner sticks with ceramic dishes manufactured in the United States.

Plastic dishes are convenient, cheap, and easy to clean but may cause some dogs to lose their nose pigment. In addition, plastic dishes aren't as durable as stainless steel or ceramic.

Deciding when to feed your dog

By making Fido's mealtimes predictable, you go a long way toward making his potty times equally predictable. You want your dog to do his bathroom business at regular, predictable intervals, which is why putting your canine housetrainee on a regular potty schedule — at least until Fido masters his bathroom basics — is a good idea. To be fully effective, that potty schedule needs to cover feeding times, because most pooches want to potty soon after they eat.

Why not free feed?

A generation ago, many people simply scooped a couple of piles of kibble into their dogs' dishes and left those dishes out all day for Fido to feast on whenever his stomach growled. Some people still do that in a practice experts call *free feeding*.

Without a doubt, free feeding is a far more convenient way to give your dog his grub than remembering to feed Fido at the same times every day. However, free feeding carries three major disadvantages, at least two of which directly affect a dog's bathroom behavior:

 ✔ **Lack of predictability:** If food is always available to your dog, you may have a tough time determining when he actually chows down. Without such knowledge, you can't really anticipate when he's likely to poop or pee. Consequently, the dog who eats whenever he wants may have more trouble learning his bathroom basics than the dog whose mealtimes are scheduled.

 ✔ **Lack of regularity:** Determining how much food a dog has eaten at any one time is tough if he has 24/7 access to that food. That means you won't realize as quickly whether your dog is eating his usual fill. That lack of knowledge may keep you from spotting potential health problems.

 ✔ **Too much autonomy:** By letting your pooch have unfettered access to food, you're foregoing important opportunities to reinforce your status as the leader. Every time your dog sees you prepare and serve him his food, he realizes that you are the Giver of All Good Things. That realization strengthens the bond you share and encourages his desire to please you, both of which help you teach him the lessons he needs to learn — including housetraining.

Setting a schedule for every dog

Frequent meals will help keep your dog in the best of health — especially if he's a young puppy. A juvenile canine needs to eat more often than an adult dog does, but even an adult dog may need to dine more often than you may suspect. Here are some various feeding schedules:

- ✔ **Puppies under 4 months:** The little ones should get at least three meals a day: morning, midday, and early evening. Make water available at mealtimes, plus for a little while after dinner. Take up the water no later than two hours before bedtime, though, or your pup will need a middle-of-the-night potty break.

- ✔ **Puppies from 4 months to 1 year:** These puppies can cut back to two meals per day: one in the morning and one in the evening. And if they've mastered Housetraining 101, they can get start getting unlimited water.

- ✔ **Adult dogs:** Adults do best with two meals a day plus unlimited water. Although many grown-up pooches do get by with just one big dinner each day, a twice-daily meal plan can help forestall a boatload of problems. For example, dogs, like people, tend to get sleepy after they eat — which means that the dog who gets a good breakfast in the morning is more likely to nap than to trash the house if his human companion is gone all day. And a good dinner will help him sleep more comfortably through the night.

The morning-and-evening regimen can also help prevent physical problems. Some, such as flatulence, usually aren't serious. But one deadly condition, *bloat,* can result if a dog scarfs down a very large meal. Large dogs are more likely to be stricken with bloat (also known as *gastric tortion*) than smaller breeds are. For more on bloat, see Chapter 10.

Before or after the humans eat?

Some people find that feeding Fido before they eat works well. They find that a dog with a full tummy is less likely to try scoring table scraps from the human family members while they eat.

Still others favor simultaneous dining: Letting the dog eat at the same time that his people do. One undeniable advantage to this option is that the dog is too busy eating her own food to worry about eating yours, at least for the first few minutes of your meal. However, the logistics of preparing human and canine cuisine at the same time can prove to be a challenge to people like me, whose multitasking ability is somewhat limited!

And some people suggest feeding your dog after the people in the house have their meals. They believe that making a dog wait for her meals underscores the fact that people outrank the pooches in the family pack. They also point out that among wolves observed in captivity, the alpha wolf generally eats before the rest of the pack does. Consequently, feed-the-dog-last advocates believe that alpha people should follow suit when feeding their canine pack members.

I don't advocate any one of these three dining options over the others. The right answer varies with each dog and each family. I generally feed my dog, Allie, before the rest of my family eats — not because she begs for table goodies (we don't permit such behavior in our house) but because the humans in our house tend to dine late. For that reason, I give my Golden girl her grub around 7:00 a.m. and 5:00 p.m.

To Treat or Not to Treat

Dogs love to snack and eat treats just as much as people do — but the question of whether to give a pooch any treats in housetraining can be difficult to answer. Certainly, you can make a good case for using treats to train your dog. They're a great learning incentive; I use them liberally when training my own dog and working with other people's pooches. You can use a treat to actually lure a dog into sitting or lying down on command (see Figure 4-1). A treat makes a great reward for the dog who's learning to come on command and can spark your dog's learning process in countless other ways.

A whole segment of expert dog trainers uses treats as the foundation of their training philosophy, known in most circles as *positive reinforcement*. Proponents of positive reinforcement rely on treats and other rewards (such as a toy and/or lavish praise) to help a dog understand what a person wants the animal to do.

Many trainers and other experts — myself included — swear by treats as an unbeatable training tool. Treats are a gentle (not to mention tasty) way to jump-start a dog's desire to learn. Just follow these guidelines to ensure that your dog's other lessons don't interfere with his lessons on proper potty protocol:

- ✔ **Teach just before mealtimes.** Give your dog his lessons in sitting, lying down, and other maneuvers just before he eats. A hungry dog has more incentive to learn than a dog whose tummy is full. And by giving him those treats just before mealtime, you probably won't have to get him to his potty immediately after his lesson. You can just feed him and bring him to his bathroom after the meal.

Figure 4-1: Treats can be a great teaching tool.

✔ **Keep treats teensy.** A housetrainee needs just a taste of his favorite treat to know when he's doing the right thing. The smaller the treat, the less chance that he'll pork out or get a digestive upset.

✔ **Adjust the main course.** Many treats — especially the commercial variety — are incredibly fattening. If you're giving your housetrainee commercial goodies during his housetraining and other lessons, you need to reduce the portions you put in his dish at mealtimes. Otherwise, your pooch will pork out quickly.

✔ **Easy does it.** If you're using treats for training, limit giving your dog extra goodies at other times — no matter how much he may beg for them.

In this section, I name some treats that may be appropriate for your dog, including some low-calorie options.

Buying commercial treats

People who decide to add treats to a dog's diet find an incredible assortment of goodies to choose from. Regular supermarket aisles, pet boutique floor space, print catalog pages, and online pet store bandwidth are clogged with culinary offerings designed to please the most discriminating canine palate. Here are some of the more common types of commercial treats:

- **Biscuits and cookies:** From the been-around-forever offerings of Del Monte's Milk-Bones to the gourmet fare of Three Dog Bakery, biscuits and cookies jump-start the appetites of countless canines. The fact that most dogs love scarfing down biscuits and cookies gives these products a big advantage. Another is that their small sizes make them easy for dogs to chew and digest. In addition, their crunchy textures provide good chewing exercise for dogs and can even help clean a canine's canines (as well as her other teeth).

  The downside? Many biscuits and cookies are loaded with calories. In addition, some treats can upset the nutritional balance that commercial dog foods offers.

  If you're worried about upsetting the nutritional balance offered by your dog's commercial food, try a treat that carries the same product name as the main food product. Science Diet (by Hills) and California Natural (by Innova) are just two product lines that include treats designed to dovetail with their regular dog foods.

- **Chew treats:** Most dogs adore chomping on chew treats made of rawhide, pigs' ears, cows' hooves, and other animal parts.

  Some dogs may adore chew treats a little too much. These chewing maniacs may gnaw off and swallow big chunks of such treats, and those chunks can cause internal injuries. For that reason, don't feed chew treats unless you can directly supervise your dog. If she has a sensitive stomach, don't offer them at all.

Hot dog! A quick and easy treat

Want to make a fast, can't-miss treat for your dog? Get some hot dogs, slice them up thin, and cook them in your microwave until they're as crisp as bacon. Afterward, drain the slices on some paper towels. Feed these to even the pickiest pooch, and he'll worship the ground you walk on — plus learn his doggie lessons faster than you dreamed possible. A treat this tasty can give your dog the incentive to pick up just about anything more quickly, including proper potty protocol. Do feed these nuked goodies sparingly, though — although hot dogs are delicious, they're not the most nutritious foods for humans or canines.

Preparing homemade treats

If you enjoy making treats for yourself and the other people in your household, you may also enjoy making treats for your canine family member. Homemade treats offer several advantages over commercial fare, the biggest being that you have much more control. When you make treats yourself, you know which ingredients (and how much of each) go into the treat — an important consideration if, for example, your canine companion suffers from food allergies. You can also control the size of the treat so that it's just right for your particular dog.

Like the idea of giving your dog homemade goodies but don't know where to begin? Type "dog treat recipes" into an Internet search engine and dig out thousands of sites that contain recipes to try on your four-legged friend. One caution, though: Most of these sites don't include any nutritional analysis — so feed sparingly, no matter how much your dog loves the results of your efforts. If you're not computer inclined, your public library undoubtedly has plenty of books on dog treats for you to peruse. Or if you want a treat recipe book of your very own, check out Liz Palika's excellent tome, *The Ultimate Dog Treat Cookbook* (Wiley).

Never give your dog anything that contains chocolate. Although most dogs like it (at least the smell!), chocolate contains an ingredient that's toxic to them. Even a small amount can put your dog in dire distress and even kill him.

Choosing low-calorie treat options

Yes, you can give your dog treats without necessarily causing him to put on excess poundage. Here are some possibilities:

- **Fruits and vegetables:** Many dogs adore raw or frozen fruits and vegetables, and because they're so low in calories, they make a terrific treat for the plumper pooch. Good veggies to try are carrots, Brussels sprouts, broccoli, and green beans. For fruits, consider apples.

Make sure that you offer small pieces of veggies and fruits so your four-legged friend can digest those greens and yellows easily. And be aware that vegetables contain fiber, which acts as a laxative. If you give your pooch too many veggies, he'll need to poop a lot more often.

Don't feed your dog grapes, raisins, or onions. They contain compounds that are toxic to dogs in sufficient quantities. Besides, who wants a dog with onion breath?

✔ **Rice cakes:** They may seem utterly devoid of taste to you, me, and other human gourmands — but believe me, I have seen otherwise discriminating dogs go nuts over the prospect of getting a piece of rice cake. One Dachshund of my acquaintance started barking madly for hers as soon as she saw one of her people getting the package out from the kitchen cabinet.

✔ **Low-cal commercial treats.** Some pet food manufacturers offer low-calorie versions of their usual dog treats. Try giving some to your dog if he doesn't go for the veggies or rice cakes.

The truth about table scraps

You see the warnings in just about every dog care book on the shelves. "Do not feed your dog table scraps!" they screech. Their reasons are virtuous and worthy: Rich, spicy food from the table gives your dog indigestion — and everyone knows what the results of *that* will be! If you give your dog scraps from the table, you'll be encouraging him to adopt the obnoxious habit of begging. And no matter how you present those scraps, you'll upset the nutritional balance of his carefully formulated dog food.

Good reasons, all. There's just one problem: Almost everyone I know gives their canine companion food from the table at one time or another. Holidays are one example. Even a pooch who's never eaten anything but dry food for dinner will turn those big-guilt-inducing eyes on her people when they sit down to an elaborate feast.

Instead of sticking with the no-table-scraps prohibition that everyone ignores, here are a few guidelines for giving your dog an occasional people-food treat:

✔ **Don't feed from the table.** The experts are right on this one; feeding anything from the table encourages your dog to beg. I don't like being stared at while I eat, and you probably don't, either. Don't let the habit start in the first place. Instead, put the goodies directly into your dog's dish.

✔ **Don't give real garbage.** You wouldn't feed yourself the germ-ridden food thrown into the garbage, would you? Well, your dog shouldn't get that food, either.

✔ **Nix fats and spices.** Foods laden with fats and spices upset your dog's stomach. Few events put more of a damper on a holiday dinner than having to clean up the results of that tummy upset, especially if that upset occurs near the dinner table. Even worse, fatty foods can induce inflammation of the pancreas — in vetspeak, *pancreatitis* — which can be a life-threatening disease. Excess salt can encourage drinking and extra potty breaks.

So which table scraps are okay? If you're sharing Thanksgiving dinner with your dog, you can safely give him a little bit of the turkey white meat (the dark meat is too fatty). Veggies please many canine palates, too; just go easy on them, or your dog will poop more than usual.

Working with Your Dog's Drinking Habits

Dogs need water for the same reasons that people do: to regulate their body temperature, to shuttle nutrients via the bloodstream from the digestive system to anywhere else the body needs them, and to transport waste products in the form of urine outside the body via urination. But although all dogs need water for the same reasons, the amount of water they need varies from pooch to pooch. Dogs who are very active and/or eat a lot of food — especially dry food — need to drink more water than more sedentary canines, those who eat less, and/or those whose diets include some canned or moist fare.

Healthy, housetrained dogs can regulate their water intake all by themselves. They drink when they're thirsty and don't drink when they're not. Meeting the water needs of these dogs is simple: Keep water available at all times.

Keeping water available does not mean just topping the water off throughout the day or week. A dog needs totally fresh water in a dish that you wash at least once a day. Change the water itself at least once a day or anytime you see stuff — for example, little bits of food residue — floating in the water.

That said, 24/7 access to water can pose a problem for the canine housetrainee. To anticipate when your dog may need to let some water out — in other words, to pee — you need to have some idea of when he took that water in. The best way to acquire that knowledge is to control his access to the water bowl. Make no mistake: The dog who's just learning basic bathroom manners needs frequent opportunities to drink. But you need to know when he takes advantage of those opportunities — and the best way to gain that knowledge is to give him a full dish of clean water several times a day — at the very least, at the same time as every meal — at the same times each and every day.

If your dog suddenly starts drinking more water than usual — and consequently starts peeing more often than usual — he may well be sick. Chapter 10 outlines some of the maladies that increased water intake may signify and what you can do about them.

Just as distilled or filtered water can improve a human being's health, so can it do good things for the health of a dog. A prime potential benefit: preventing the formation of certain types of bladder stones, which can be life-threatening if left untreated. Distilled or filtered water doesn't contain any of the minerals that cause stones to form.

Part II
Putting a Plan in Place

The 5th Wave   By Rich Tennant

"You know, you're never going to get that dog to do her business in your remote control dump truck."

In this part...

Here's where you begin to housetrain your dog in earnest. This part gives you detailed directions on teaching your dog to love the crate and explains how to train her to do her business indoors or outdoors. You also discover how to figure out when your dog's trying to tell you that she needs to go, how to deal with mistakes, and how to tell when your four-legged friend is really, truly housetrained.

Chapter 5

Training to Love the Crate

*T*he crate is crucial not only to successful housetraining but also, in my view, to successful puppy-raising. Not only does a crate capitalize on your pooch's instinctive desire not to dirty her den — and thus learn to hold her poop and pee until she can do so in the right place — but it also gives you a safe place to put your puppy when you can't keep your eye on her, including while you sleep at night. And believe me, a puppy (or in many cases, even an adult dog) needs a human's eagle eye to prevent her from engaging in mischief such as unfurling the toilet paper, diving into the garbage, or chewing on the legs of your dining room chairs.

But the crate's benefits extend not only to you; they also include your four-legged friend. The crate is a place where your dog can retreat whenever she needs a break from everyday household mayhem, wants a little alone time, or needs to escape from what she perceives to be big, bad, scary machinery such as vacuum cleaners.

Unfortunately, though, the benefits of crates may not be readily apparent to your canine companion — at least not at first. Instead of considering it to be her own special space, a dog may view the crate as a canine prison to which she's received a lifetime sentence. That's why you can't simply put your dog into the crate, shut the door, and walk away any more than you can teach a child to swim by bringing him to deep water and then expecting him to paddle his way back to shore.

You need to introduce your canine companion to her crate carefully. This chapter helps you do just that, and it also gives you some ideas for helping your canine companion change her mind about her crate if she already hates it. (For info on selecting and outfitting a crate and deciding where to put it, go to Chapter 3.)

Introducing the Crate

To help your canine companion appreciate her crate, introduce her to it immediately but gradually. If possible, start on the very same day you welcome her into your home. In this section, I explain what to do as you introduce your dog to her crate. This process should take only a day or two, unless your four-legged friend has had a prior negative experience with the crate. If that's the case with your dog, expect the process to take longer.

Tie one on: The open-door policy

No, no, no — I am not suggesting that the way to help your dog learn to love her crate is for you to head around the corner to the nearest pub and party hearty. Instead, you need to make the crate, particularly the door, nonthreatening to your four-legged friend. A door that suddenly slams shut while your dog is getting accustomed to the crate can spook your pooch into bypassing the crate completely.

Before you introduce the crate to your little Fidette, use a string or a prop to keep the crate door open. That way, when she explores the crate, a sudden accidental slamming of the door won't put your pup off the crate.

Encourage exploration

As soon as you have the crate door securely open, encourage your puppy or dog to check out the crate. Begin by letting her walk around the crate to sniff and otherwise explore it. If she hesitates, throw little treats around the perimeter.

When your puppy approaches the crate comfortably, see whether you can induce her to venture inside the crate — again with the help of a tasty treat. If your housetrainee isn't food-motivated, a favorite toy may do the trick. Either way, toss the treat or toy inside the crate. If she goes in readily, praise her; if she's hesitant, tell her in a high, happy-sounding voice to go and get the goodies.

Don't force her in; let her decide on her own to enter the crate. And when she does, let her know what a good girl she is. This may take some time; be prepared to spend an afternoon or so helping her with this crucial step.

Nighty-night: Getting your dog to go in her den when asked

When I was housetraining Allie, my Golden Retriever, I ended up teaching her something else without even realizing it: going into her crate when asked.

That's because every time I put Allie into her crate, I would tell her "nighty-night" in a soft, baby-talk sort of voice. Before very long, Allie figured out all by herself that "nighty-night" meant that it was time for her to head to her crate. Even now, six years later, if I tell her, "Allie, time to go nighty-night," my Golden girl trots into her crate, no matter where she is in our house.

The nighty-night maneuver comes in handy if, for example, you have a repair person coming into your house and you don't want Daisy and the repair person to meet. In fact, for any situation in which you need to confine your dog, the ability to send your dog to her crate on command is a useful skill.

Of course, you don't need to use the term *nighty-night* to get your dog to head to her crate on cue. Other words work just as well. I just love to see my big 70-pound Golden girl — who at most times is quite the diva and has a mind of her own — walk with such docility into her crate while I coo "nighty-night" to her.

Whenever your puppy enters the crate (or whenever you put her in it), use a word that tells her what she's doing and where she's going. Good choices are *crate, place, bed,* or any other word that you know you'll use consistently. By saying this same word in a high, happy tone of voice whenever your dog enters her crate, you'll help her associate the word with the crate — and as I explain in the sidebar titled "Nighty-Night: Getting your dog to go in her den when asked," she'll soon begin to head into the crate as soon as you, well, say the word.

Shut the door (but not for long)

If your puppy repeatedly enters her crate without hesitation, untie the door. Toss a treat inside the crate. When your pooch enters, shut the door quietly without locking it. Leave it shut for just a few seconds.

During those few seconds, praise your pooch lavishly, and then open the door and coax her out. Another tiny treat should provide sufficient incentive for her to emerge.

Perform this sequence five to ten times during the day, gradually increasing the amount of time the door remains closed, until your puppy is able to remain calmly in the crate for about 5 minutes.

No dishes? No problem!

Maybe your dog's crate doesn't come with dishes, or maybe you just find them too cumbersome, messy, or awkward to use. That's okay. You have another option for keeping your dog occupied while she's in the crate: filling an interactive toy with food and/or treats.

Take a toy such as a Kong (you can find one at any pet supply store or at the Kong Web site, www.kongcompany.com) or other food-dispensing plaything and slather some peanut butter on the inside. Then fill the toy with treats, or even regular food, and pack it tight. Put the stuffed toy inside your pooch's crate. Chances are, she'll make a beeline for the toy, get immediately to work trying to ferret out the goodies you've shoehorned into it, and not even notice that you've closed the door.

If you really want to challenge your housetrainee, put the treat-stuffed toy in a plastic bag and into your freezer for a couple of hours. Then remove it from the freezer, take the toy out of the bag, and hand it over to your dog, who by now is probably salivating. The food stuffed inside the toy will be even tougher for your four-legged friend to extract.

This trick works not only for crate training but also for other training situations. For example, dogs with separation anxiety often do very well if their owners give them food-stuffed interactive toys just before they leave the house. The dogs are so engrossed in getting the goodies that they don't even realize their people have left — and afterward, their contented tummies may well induce them to take a post-snacking nap.

Of course, if you make a regular practice of giving your pooch a meal in one of her toys, make sure you adjust her other meal portions accordingly. That way, she'll retain her girlish figure as she works her way to becoming a housetraining graduate.

Leave the room

After your puppy can stay calmly in the crate for 5 minutes, you're ready for the next step, which is to have her stay calmly in her crate without you there. Once again, lure your pooch into her crate — but this time, use something more substantial than a treat or two. A full meal dispensed into a crate dish is a good choice (or use a food-stuffed toy — see the sidebar titled "No dishes? No problem!" for details).

When your pup is in her crate, shut the door quietly and leave the room for about a minute. When you return, see what your puppy's doing. If she's eating her meal or gnawing her chew toy contentedly, leave the room again and come back in a few more minutes. Keep checking until she's finished; when she's done, let her out of the crate and praise her lavishly for her accomplishment. Give her a special treat to emphasize to her how pleased you are.

Build up her tolerance

You're now ready for the final step in your puppy's Loving the Crate 101 course: building up her tolerance for being in the crate by herself. This one should be easy: Keep feeding her inside the crate until she's able to stay in it for half an hour. Then try leaving the house for a few minutes, gradually extending the time that you're away. At this point, she should handle crate time without any problem.

If, at any point in this process, your dog starts to whine or cry, you may be moving too quickly. Help for the whiny crate trainee appears in the next section.

Encouraging Appreciation If Your Dog Hates the Crate

Alas, not every dog appreciates a crate. An adult dog who's never been inside a crate may think it's a prison, not a haven. A puppy-mill pooch who spent his babyhood cramped inside a crate that was too small and who was forced to eliminate while inside that crate may not think the crate you've purchased is such a great idea, either.

Either way, a dog who hesitates to enter a crate for the first time probably just needs some patience from you and a clear incentive to give the crate a try. Find a treat that your dog is passionate about and hold it to his nose so that he knows what's being offered. Then use a high-pitched, happy-sounding tone of voice to encourage him to enter the crate. As soon as he makes the big step and ventures inside the crate, praise him to the skies. Above all, don't shut the door until he's going in and out of the crate without hesitation.

Some dogs balk when they're left alone in the crate for the first time. If that's the case with your pooch, stay away for just a minute or so after he starts fussing. Then come back into the room and reassure him with a quick "good boy" or "good dog." Leave the room again for just a few seconds — and if he stays quiet for that brief time, come back to let him out of the crate and praise him. The important thing here is not to let him out of the crate until he stops fussing.

Not on my bed, you don't

When President Obama and his family first acquired Bo, their Portuguese Water Dog, a reporter asked the president whether Bo would sleep on any of the White House beds. The Chief Executive's firm response was, "Not on *my* bed." He also indicated that the First Dog would not be sleeping on either of his daughters' beds, either. Bo is the first dog the Obamas have owned, but they've made the right decision in opting to keep Bo off their beds.

Puppies and human beds don't mix for several reasons. First, there's the possibility that the puppy will wander from where he's sleeping to somewhere else on your bed and decide (yuck) to do his business there. Second, he could fall off the bed and hurt himself. And third, it sets a bad precedent for a relationship in which you're trying to establish yourself as his leader — a loving, benevolent leader but a leader nevertheless.

So what should you do if your puppy balks at being in his crate at night? Here are some ideas:

- **Keep the crate in your bedroom.** Just because you don't allow your dog on your bed doesn't mean that he can't sleep in the same room with you. Simply bring the crate into your bedroom with you at bedtime. For many puppies and dogs, simply being in the same room as their people is enough to calm them and allow everyone to get a good night's sleep.

- **Dangle your fingers.** For a few people-loving puppies, being in their humans' bedrooms doesn't offer enough proximity to their humans. (My Allie was one of these puppies.) If that's the case with your new four-legged friend, bring his crate right up next to your bed and dangle your fingers in front of the crate door every time he cries. Chances are, he'll sniff your fingers and quiet down.

- **Stay positive.** Scolding your puppy, using a shake can, banging on the crate, or any other negative response to his whining usually won't keep him quiet — or if it does, not for very long. Staying positive helps him associate the crate with pleasant occurrences.

- **Check the time.** If your puppy continues to cry — and if he's under 4 months of age — he may need a potty break. Most puppies younger than 4 months can't hold it all night long. Take a look at what time it is: If your puppy's whining any time after 2 a.m. or so and several hours have passed since his previous pit stop, haul yourself out of bed and take him to his potty spot.

Many young puppies object to being put in crates at night during their first few nights in a new home. They cry pitifully and otherwise carry on, tempting their soft-hearted people to scoop them out of their crates and allow them to sleep with them in their own beds. This is a temptation that you should do your very best not to give in to. The nearby sidebar titled "Not on my bed, you don't" explains why and provides advice for dealing with this common situation.

If you've done your best but there's no way your dog will accept the crate, don't despair. For a few pooches, particularly puppy-mill dogs and their offspring, as well as dogs who suffer from severe separation anxiety, the crate will never be the cozy den it represents to the vast majority of canines. For these dogs, the solution is to create an indoor home-alone area that's less enclosed than a crate is but still protects your home while the dogs learn proper potty protocol. Suggestions for creating this special indoor potty are in Chapter 11.

 A dog who suffers from separation anxiety — in other words, panics and becomes destructive when left alone — can benefit from professional help. An experienced trainer can help you teach your anxious pooch that solitude is okay. In severe cases, a veterinarian can prescribe medication that helps to lessen the dog's anxiety.

Limiting Crate Time: How Much Is Too Much?

As you've undoubtedly discovered, I'm a passionate advocate of *crate training,* keeping your four-legged friend in her doggie den whenever you can't watch her directly and letting her out for mealtimes, potty breaks, and playtime. Nothing, in my view, makes the whole teaching Doggie Bathroom Manners 101 process easier than having a crate that capitalizes on your dog's instinctive desire to keep her den clean. But that said, it's entirely possible that use of a crate can be too much of a good thing — and even cruel to your four-legged friend.

Too many people embrace the crate a little too tightly and turn it into a canine warehouse. They put their dogs into their crates in the morning, go out all day, and then come home in the evening to let their pooches out. Yes, the furniture and rugs are free of destruction, dog poop, and other hazards that are part of sharing one's life with a dog. But confining your dog to a crate for that long is inhumane — even if she can hold it all day.

Not only does crating your dog for too long cause her discomfort in bowel and bladder — possibly even causing a urinary tract infection — but you also deprive your dog of exercise, mental stimulation, and your company, all of which can cause her to develop a distaste for her crate. And if she can't hold her poop and pee, you've really made things tough for her, because you've forced her to dirty her den and then stay in that dirt until you let her out.

Generally, I don't think it's fair to confine even a fully housetrained dog to a crate for more than 4 or 5 hours at a time. And as you can see in Chapters 6 and 7, dogs who are still developing their basic bathroom manners need to be let out of their crates much more often. That said, it's okay to crate a dog overnight after she's demonstrated that she can hold it for that long (generally after a puppy reaches 4 months of age). But keep that crate with you in your bedroom so she can share space with you and you can hear her if she has a problem or needs a middle-of-the-night pit stop after all (for example, if she's suffering from a urinary infection or diarrhea).

If you think your schedule or your home décor requires all-day crate confinement for your dog, you need to explore other options. Here's what you can do:

- ✔ **Come home at lunch.** If your workplace is close to your home, make a quick trip there during your lunch break to give your four-legged friend a much-needed potty break.

- ✔ **Hire a dog walker.** Urban and suburban areas abound with pet sitters and dog walkers who are more than happy to spring your pooch each day for a reasonable fee. Check out your newspaper classifieds, your veterinarian's office, or an online source such as Craigslist (www.craigslist.org).

- ✔ **Enlist a neighbor.** If you have a dog-loving neighbor who stays home during the day, maybe she'd be willing to come visit your dog and walk him at noontime. Of course, if you embark on such an arrangement, make sure that you're willing to offer her services that she needs, such as watering her plants and picking up her mail whenever she goes away.

- ✔ **Bring your pooch to work.** Many workplaces allow their employees to bring their well-behaved dogs to work. Check with your company's human resources department to see whether your company is one of these dog-friendly treasures. If so, you can take your-legged friend out of his crate periodically for a walk and a potty break.

- ✔ **Consider doggie day care.** More and more cities and towns offer cage-free doggie day care to give the confined canine a more pleasurable day. See whether yours is one of them.

Continuing to Use the Crate

After your dog becomes a fan of the crate, you can adopt a few measures to help her keep those good feelings. Crates have many benefits beyond housetraining, so maintaining that appreciation is well worth the effort. In this section, I explain how to do just that, and I name some other ways you and your canine companion can use the crate.

Keeping the love alive

You need to do your part to make sure that the crate continues to be something your dog loves. Here are some ways to do just that:

✔ **Potty first.** If you plan to have your puppy or dog stay in her crate while you leave the house, give her an opportunity to poop or pee beforehand. A before-the-crate bathroom break greatly decreases the odds that your four-legged friend will go to the bathroom while she's in the crate.

✔ **Let her settle.** If you're crating your puppy or dog in her crate while you go out to run errands, put her there a few minutes before you depart. That way, she'll have a chance to settle herself before you head out the door.

✔ **Downplay comings and goings.** Don't make a big deal of putting your dog in her crate when you leave or of letting her out when you arrive home. Big, emotional hellos and goodbyes can put your dog on emotional overload, making settling down in the crate tougher for her to handle.

✔ **Potty last.** Just as you took her to her potty before you left, do the same thing when you arrive home. A dog who's held her poop and pee while crated needs and deserves the consideration of a bathroom break as soon as possible thereafter.

Beyond housetraining: Other uses for the crate

Even after your puppy or dog is housetrained, you and your dog will still find the crate useful. Here are some other roles a crate can play:

✔ **A room of her own:** In addition to using the crate as a safe place in which to avoid fearsome vacuum cleaners and get herself some space during my family's TV time, my Allie occasionally uses her crate as a place to stash toys and treats. (Unfortunately, she soon forgets that she's done so.)

✔ **A place away from visitors:** The crate's a great place for your dog to stay if you have repair personnel or other visitors come into your home. Even if your dog is a social butterfly, your guests may appreciate not having to deal with sloppy doggie kisses and shedding. And if your dog is more reserved, she'll appreciate having a place to retreat to when strangers come around.

✔ **A safe way to travel:** The crate is a safe place for your dog to be when you're both traveling by car — and it's required if you're both traveling by air and the dog is too large to join you in the passenger cabin.

✔ **A home away from home:** Many hotels and motels that generally frown on accommodating animals may cut you a break if you can tell them your dog will be crated. And if you think that you'll visit only pet-friendly hotels, well, you may not have that option. If you and your dog find yourselves having to leave your home to outrun a natural disaster such as a hurricane, having a crate can save the day (not to mention your pet's life) when you're both scrambling to find a safe shelter.

Crates are also great when you're visiting relatives or friends in their homes and want to bring your dog along. She'll be a lot more comfortable having a familiar home away from home, and your hosts will be more comfortable knowing that your dog has a place to be that will keep her from damaging their stuff.

✔ **A place to heal:** The crate may serve as a recovery room for your dog if she undergoes orthopedic surgery such as anterior cruciate ligament (ACL) repair (a common problem that big dogs such as Labrador Retrievers face). In fact, many veterinarians require that their canine ACL patients be on what they call *crate rest* for at least several weeks after surgery. Under such circumstances, the dog who's accustomed staying in her crate and liking it will fare far better than her crate-hating counterpart. The same situation applies if your dog is being treated for heartworm.

Any way you look at the crate, though, the bottom line is that a dog who has gotten a good start with one is probably going to have a good start with housetraining and every other kind of training. Showing your dog that her crate is something to love is worth every bit of effort you and she make.

Chapter 6

Heading to the Outside: Outdoor Housetraining

*I*f you're like most people, you're planning to teach your puppy or adult dog to do his business outdoors. There's one very good reason to consider keeping a dog's bathroom business outdoors: not wanting to deal with dog doo inside one's house.

Face it: No one truly likes to deal with canine waste (I'm having fun writing about it, but that's a whole other issue). Doggie doo stinks, and so does doggie pee. Plus, both stain any fabrics that they touch. Worst of all, dog poop is full of germs, bacteria, and other unlovely organisms that can literally sicken both you and your dog.

Beyond the obvious, though, are plenty of other good reasons to teach a dog to limit his bathroom maneuvers to outdoor turf. For one thing, the owner of an outdoor-trained dog doesn't have to allocate one bit of floor space to newspapers, litter boxes, or other types of dog potties. In addition, the outdoor potty can go just about anywhere that you and your dog go; all you need are some bags with which to perform cleanup. Finally, outdoor time with your dog is good for both your mental health and his.

This chapter shows you how to teach your dog to potty outdoors, no matter what his age.

Understanding How Outdoor Training Works

Outdoor training is the process of teaching your dog to eliminate only when he's outside. You can consider your pooch to be successfully outdoor-trained if she consistently holds her poop and pee until you take her outside — or if she takes herself there.

Achieving such success can be surprisingly simple. Every time you think your dog needs a potty break, you take her outside to her potty spot to do her business. At first, you do this according to a set schedule. Sometimes, though, your dog needs to diverge from that schedule — and in all likelihood, she'll communicate somehow that she needs to go. (Chapter 8 tells you how she's most likely to communicate that need and how you can teach her to ask you for a bathroom break in a way that you'll readily understand.)

At all other times, you either confine her to her crate or watch her continuously for those pre-potty communications. The objectives here are to prevent accidents from occurring and to encourage your dog to do her business outdoors — and outdoors only. Within a matter of weeks, she understands that it's okay to potty outside and takes it upon herself to make sure that she doesn't eliminate inside.

Outdoor training needn't be difficult, but it does require time, attention, and patience from you. Training puppies takes a little more work than training an adult dog — for one thing, puppies need more potty breaks — but either way, you can introduce your dog to her potty spot, set up a schedule, and get training off to a good start.

Introducing Puppies to Outdoor Training

The great thing about outdoor training is that you can start doing it right away. And if you're really lucky, your puppy's breeder has started the process for you. In this section, you find out how to show your dog his potty spot, how to encourage your dog with verbal cues, and how to develop a pup-sized training schedule.

Getting an early start

Many breeders start introducing puppies to doing their business outdoors when the pups reach the age of 4 or 5 weeks. This is the time when the mama dog starts to push the puppies out of the den so that they don't do their business anywhere nearby. A good breeder often gives the mother some help by taking the puppies outside in nice weather and encouraging them to eliminate there.

If your breeder hasn't started outdoor training, or if your puppy comes from an animal shelter or rescue group, you can set the process in motion even before you and your puppy hit the road and head for home. Start by asking for a piece of paper towel or cloth that's scented with a bit of the pup's urine. You'll use this pre-scented cloth to help your puppy figure out where he can potty.

Taking the first trips outside

Housetraining can and should start as soon as you bring your new friend home. In this section, I describe when and how the first outdoor bathroom breaks should occur.

Visiting the potty spot after the ride home

As soon as you and your puppy arrive home for the first time, take your puppy to the outdoor potty area you've chosen (see Chapter 3 for tips on choosing one). Car rides often trigger a puppy's I-gotta-go-right-now reflex, so let him do the doo and/or take a whiz before you head into the house. Place a cloth scented with your puppy's urine on the ground and let your puppy sniff it. Then, when your puppy opens his floodgates and/or makes a solid deposit, praise him enthusiastically. Let him know that he's done exactly what you wanted him to do. (Check out the later section "Responding when your puppy potties" for details.)

If he doesn't go, give him a little more time to explore. And even if he does eliminate, don't head back into the house right away. Many puppies need to pee two or three times during a potty break before they're completely empty.

If the outdoor potty area is in an unfenced area of your yard, leash your puppy before taking him to do the doo.

Taking your pup out after he sees the house

After your puppy does his business outdoors, take your puppy inside and let him explore your abode for a little while — but keep an eagle eye trained on your new friend. You need to watch for any signal that he's about to do a repeat potty performance. Here are some signs he's just seconds away from unloading:

- ✔ He calls a sudden halt to his investigations.
- ✔ He begins to sniff in a direct and purposeful manner.
- ✔ He starts walking around in a circle.
- ✔ He actually begins to drop his bottom downward.

Quickly — and I do mean *quickly* — scoop him up and take him outside to the same spot he anointed or pooped on earlier. The odor of his previous encounter will probably prompt him to perform an encore there. When he does, praise him and give him a treat.

If for some reason you don't see any signs that he's about to go and he surprises you with a little puddle or pile, say nothing. Simply clean up the mess — and promise yourself that you'll watch your little darling more carefully in the future. (Meanwhile, check out Chapter 8, which describes pre-potty signals in detail.)

After your puppy explores his new home for about an hour, he'll probably be pretty tired. Put him in his crate so he can snooze for a little while. Do keep an eye on him, though, so you can see when he wakes up. That's because a puppy who's just up from a nap is often a puppy who needs to pee. Take your little sleepyhead to his potty spot, and when he does his business, praise him and give him a tiny treat.

For your puppy's first day or two in your home, take him out every hour or two. After you're familiar with his habits, you can set up a schedule, as I discuss later in "A matter of timing: Setting up a puppy potty schedule."

Responding when your puppy potties

The way you behave while your puppy potties can either speed up or slow down his outdoor housetraining progress. That's because puppies have very short attention spans, and they can have a hard time staying focused during their potty breaks. Your behavior can either help your little guy get down to business or make him forget to do his business.

Going out to the potty spot

To help your puppy concentrate on bathroom activities, get him thinking about those activities before you reach the potty spot. As the two of you head out to your pup's bathroom, ask him, "Do you want to go potty?" or announce to him, "It's potty time!" in a lively, can't-wait-to-get-out-there tone. Use the same expression and same tone of voice every time you take little Fido out, and soon he'll associate both with heading out to the bathroom.

Take the fastest, most direct route to the potty area and use the same route every time your puppy needs a bathroom break. Your consistency conditions little Fido to expect that when he treads that path, he's going to eliminate shortly thereafter.

 As you go to the potty spot, make sure you don't walk him anywhere near the mailbox or your prize rhododendron. The dog should not be allowed to pee just anywhere, particularly in the housetraining process. Even after your dog is housetrained, if you're walking him outside, keep him off other people's lawns and confine his bathroom activities to the median strip between the sidewalk and street.

 Have treats at the ready — in your coat pocket, in a small dish from which you can grab one or two — so you'll be able to give your puppy one of those treats while the two of you are outdoors. It's important to reward him immediately after he does his good deed so that he associates the reward with the deed.

Letting your pup do his business

When the two of you arrive at the potty spot, don't do anything. Don't talk to your puppy and don't play with him until he's figured out where he's going to go and is clearly about to do so. Let him walk around a little bit — no farther than the length of a 6-foot leash — and don't let him leave the area until he's unloaded.

 As your little guy squats (male puppies don't start lifting their legs to pee until they're older, and most females never do), give him a command such as "Go potty" or "Do your business." Repeat this phrase every time he eliminates. By doing so, you up your puppy's chances of learning to pee and poop on command — a handy skill for him to have. (More info on how to teach your dog to poop and pee on command — and what to do if he's one of those dogs who can't or won't acquire this skill — is in Chapter 8.)

As soon as your puppy is finished, praise him for his performance in a high, happy-sounding voice (but don't get too loud, or you may scare the little guy). Give him a very small treat, take him for a walk, play with him, and indulge in a love fest. You've both earned it!

What if he doesn't go?

Sometimes, a puppy just won't eliminate — even though you think it's time for him to do some doo. If you've been out for more than five minutes and your puppy hasn't pooped or peed, take him back inside. But watch him like a hawk; don't take your eyes off him. Look for signs that he needs to go: circling, pacing, intense sniffing, a sudden stop in the middle of an activity. The second you see any such signs, get him back outside. If you can't watch him, put him in his crate.

Whether he's in his crate or out on the floor with you, take him out again after 20 minutes. If he goes, praise him, treat him, and take him back inside for some supervised playtime. If he doesn't go, put him back in his crate, wait another 20 minutes or so, and head back outside. Eventually he *will* go; he can't hold that poop or pee forever. Praise him lavishly and give him a teensy treat when he finally does unload.

A matter of timing: Setting up a puppy potty schedule

Putting your puppy on a regular potty schedule can shorten his housetraining learning curve considerably. Your pup, even at his young age, is a creature of habit. He learns through repetition. If you take him out to pee and poop at the same times each and every day, his body will become accustomed to that schedule. He'll be conditioned to do his business at the times you want him to do it.

A regular potty schedule also eases your job as your dog's caregiver. That's because a change in a dog's regular bathroom behavior often signals that he's sick. But if your dog potties unpredictably, you won't be able to pick up any such signals.

During your puppy's first few days at home, you should note — preferably in writing if your memory is anywhere near as bad as mine is — when he goes and whether he poops, pees, or does both. You're likely to see a pattern emerge that can help you anticipate when your new family member needs to eliminate. You can use that knowledge to create a sleeping, feeding, and bathroom schedule to help your four-legged friend become a housetraining expert in a surprisingly short time.

When you put together a potty schedule for your puppy, keep in mind that most juvenile canines need to poop and/or pee at the following times:

- ✔ First thing in the morning
- ✔ Last thing at night
- ✔ During the night (if the puppy is under 4 months of age)
- ✔ After energetic playing
- ✔ After being confined in a crate
- ✔ After a nap
- ✔ After chewing on a toy or a bone
- ✔ A few minutes after eating

Armed with this knowledge, along with your observations of your dog's individual potty pattern, you can create a schedule that gives your puppy enough time to pee or poop and also gives you some predictability. Table 6-1 shows how you may structure a schedule for a 3-month-old pup. Note that all trips outside are just to the potty spot — the puppy should come inside after he's finished unloading. Note, too, that puppies younger than 3 months are likely to need go out more often. (This schedule requires someone to be home during the day to give the puppy daytime potty breaks. If you can't be your little darling's daytime bathroom escort, check out Chapter 11.)

Table 6-1	Outdoor Training Schedule for a 3-Month-Old Puppy
Time	**Tasks**
7:00 a.m.	Take puppy outside. Feed puppy. Offer water. Take puppy outside. Play with puppy up to 15 minutes. Take puppy outside. Put puppy in crate.
Midmorning	Take puppy outside. Offer water. Play with puppy up to 15 minutes. Take puppy outside. Put puppy in crate.

(continued)

Table 6-1 *(continued)*

Time	Tasks
Noon	Take puppy outside. Feed puppy. Offer water. Take puppy outside. Play with puppy 15 to 30 minutes. Take puppy outside. Put puppy in crate.
Midafternoon	Take puppy outside. Offer water. Play with puppy up to 15 minutes. Take puppy outside. Put puppy in crate.
5:30 p.m.	Take puppy outside. Feed puppy. Offer water. Take puppy outside. Play with puppy up to 1 hour and/or let puppy hang out with the family in the kitchen.
7:00 p.m.	Take puppy outside. Play with puppy up to 15 minutes. Put puppy in crate.
Before bed	Take puppy outside. Put puppy in crate.
During the night	Take puppy outside if necessary.

You may be groaning inwardly at the prospect of having to take your four-legged friend outside for a middle-of-the-night potty break. Alas, that's one of the few disadvantages of raising a puppy instead of an adult dog. A canine youngster who's under 3 or 4 months of age just can't hold his poop or pee for the entire night any more than a human infant can sleep through the night without filling his diaper. So when your puppy fidgets, whines, or cries in the middle of night, know that he probably has a very good reason to do so. Heed his plea and take him out.

Know that as your puppy gets older, he won't need to go outside in the middle of the night. The same will be true of the midmorning, midafternoon, and 7:00 p.m. pit stops, as well as the noontime feeding. Think twice, though, about giving him unsupervised freedom in your house, even if he's completely housetrained. Chapter 8 details how quickly you should give your juvenile housetrainee run of your premises.

Scheduling Outdoor Training for Adult Dogs

Teaching an adult dog to do her bathroom business outside is similar to teaching a puppy. The difference between the two is that the adult dog doesn't need nearly as many bathroom breaks as a puppy does. But the principles and procedures are the same: showing your four-legged friend that her bathroom is outside and doing whatever it takes to keep her from eliminating inside (see the earlier section "Introducing Puppies to Outdoor Training" for details).

Table 6-2 shows a sample schedule for outdoor-training an adult dog. As soon as your adult dog has mastered her housetraining basics — which can happen in just a few days — you can eliminate the noontime potty break and consider giving her a little more freedom in your home.

Table 6-2   Outdoor Training Schedule for an Adult Dog

Time	Tasks
7:00 a.m.	Get up. Take dog outside. Feed dog. Offer water. Take dog outside. Play with dog up to 15 minutes. Put dog in crate.
Noon	Take dog outside. Offer water. Play with dog 15 to 30 minutes. Put dog in crate.
5:30 p.m.	Take dog outside. Feed dog. Offer water. Play with dog for 1 hour and/or let her hang out with the family in the kitchen.
7:00 p.m.	Remove water.
Before bed	Take dog outside. Put dog in crate.

Dealing with Boo-boos

Yes, I know: Your puppy or dog is the most wonderful creature ever to have graced the planet (aside from yourself, your spouse, and your kids). But alas, even this paragon is not perfect; she makes mistakes — and many occur during the housetraining process. Despite your best efforts to teach her bathroom manners, your four-legged friend may not understand immediately what she's supposed to do or not do. She'll demonstrate that lack of understanding by pooping or peeing inside your home instead of outside in her designated potty area.

In this section, I tell you how to respond to bathroom boo-boos, whether you spot your dog in a squat or find a puddle or pile already on the floor.

Catching your dog in the act

If you come upon your four-legged friend starting to perform that unmistakable potty squat, you have a superb teachable moment. Your objective here: Divert your dog from doing the doo in the wrong place and put her in a position to do it the right place.

Distract your dog from making the wrong move by offering a tiny treat or a toy, clapping your hands, or saying "Oops!" in a cheerful voice. As you do so, hustle her outside to her potty spot as quickly as possible so she can finish what she started but do so in the right place. After she unloads there, praise her lavishly and give her a couple of additional treats.

Finding messes: Don't scold — just clean 'em up!

Potty mistakes try the soul of even the most patient dog owner. But no matter how irritated you feel, it's crucial to the ultimate success of your housetraining venture not to take your frustration out on your outdoor trainee. Take a deep breath and remind yourself that any mistakes she makes are *not* her fault, and don't scold her in any way. Instead, take your little transgressor back to her crate so you can concentrate on cleanup, but don't say anything to her.

After your four-legged friend is safely confined in her doggie den, grab some paper towels and some pet stain remover. Follow the directions on the cleaner bottle and completely clean up the evidence of your puppy's doo-doo boo-boo. Take her out when you've cleaned up completely, have calmed down, and can watch her.

Please, please, please do not try to correct your erring pooch by scolding her, punishing her, or rubbing her nose in her transgression. Any after-the-fact corrective efforts will be lost on her.

Folded-down ears, a tail between the legs, and a refusal to look at you do not indicate that your dog feels bad about her bathroom boo-boo. The body language you're seeing shows that she feels uneasy, distressed, or maybe even scared because of the body language that you're exhibiting. But guilty? Nope.

So if your dog doesn't understand what she's done and doesn't feel any guilt, what should you do? Simple: Just clean up the mess. Then figure out where you went wrong, as I explain in the next section.

Preventing further accidents

After you clean up a pile or puddle, think about what happened and who should take the blame for your four-legged friend's mistake. Here's a hint: Instead of focusing on your dog, focus on yourself. If she peed in your living room, ask yourself what she was doing in the living room unattended in the first place. If she pooped on your kitchen floor, ask yourself when her last bowel movement was and whether you should've anticipated that by getting her outside earlier. In other words, try to figure out what you could've done to prevent your dog's accident and what you can do to make sure that she doesn't do an encore. Table 6-3 can help you get started.

Table 6-3	Troubleshooting Your Dog's Accident
What Your Dog Did	*What You Can Do*
She peed when your back was turned.	Never let her out of her crate or living area unless you're prepared to watch her every minute.
She peed or pooped in her crate.	Make sure her crate isn't too big for her; it should be just large enough for her to stand up and turn around. Make sure, too, that she's not left in the crate for too long — three to four hours, max.

(continued)

Table 6-3 *(continued)*

What Your Dog Did	What You Can Do
She pooped without warning.	Observe what she does immediately before she makes a deposit. That way, you'll be able to scoop her up and take her outside before she has an accident.
She pees on the same indoor spot daily.	Make sure you clean up completely. And don't give your dog too much indoor freedom too soon.

Any canine potty accident contains a lesson — but the lesson is for you, not your dog. By figuring out where you went wrong and making sure that you don't make the same mistake again, you'll make a giant leap toward having a truly housetrained dog.

Of course, not all accidents occur because you weren't watching. For advice on treating special potty problems, such as wetting the bed or marking territory with urine, see Chapter 9. And for info on how bathroom behavior may be related to health problems, check out Chapter 10.

Providing Indoor Potty Areas for Outdoor Trainees

Can you successfully introduce your dog to both the outdoor potty and the indoor potty when he's a puppy who's just figuring out basic bathroom protocol? Alas, the answer seems to be a resounding no for any canine genius.

Having an indoor/outdoor dog sounds wonderfully convenient in theory, but it isn't worth trying to attain in practice. In your efforts to achieve convenience, you'll probably just confuse your four-legged friend. A dog who's confused about his household's bathroom rules often expresses his confusion by having multiple accidents in the wrong places and not knowing what he's supposed to do when you take him to the right place. Such confusion is totally unnecessary. All you need to do is decide whether you want your dog to do his business inside or outside and train him accordingly.

Resisting the allure of indoor/outdoor training

After I've gotten my weekly TV fix of *Top Chef, Project Runway,* or *Make Me a Supermodel* (and if you're reading this book after those shows have been canceled, rest assured that I'll have found new shows to replace them), the last thing I want to do is to take Allie out for her final whiz of the day. After all, it's 11 p.m. or later. I'm generally pretty tired by then. Most of the time I can guilt my husband into doing the job, even though he's not thrilled with doing it, either. And if the weather's not to Allie's liking, our distaste for the late-night potty break increases. At those times, both my spouse and I fervently wish that we could just spread some newspapers in my kitchen or basement, march Allie over to them, tell her to do her bathroom business right there (and right away), and know that she'd comply.

But we never do it. We realize that Allie wouldn't have a clue about why I'm spreading out those newspapers. She'd bypass them completely. Instead, she'd either have an accident in the house or (more likely) try to demonstrate that her bladder is made of iron. Either way, the result would not be good. If she had an accident in the house, I'd be angry about having to clean it up, even though I'd have no one to blame but myself. If she tried to hold it, she'd boost her odds of getting a urinary tract infection — which would cause her some discomfort and force me to take her to the vet for an exam and some antibiotics.

That's why, no matter how tired I am and/or how awful the weather is outside, either my husband or I take Allie out just before bedtime. We all sleep better afterward, even if it takes us a little longer to get to bed.

However, there *is* at least one situation in which you may need to provide a temporary indoor potty for your outdoor trainee: if you're out all day and have a puppy who's less than around 5 months of age. A dog this young simply can't hold it from nine to five, and even asking him to try is wrong.

If your ultimate goal is to train your puppy to potty only outdoors, both you and he will be better off if you can find a way to give your puppy a midday potty break (see Chapter 5 for some of your options). But if none of those options is feasible, you must let your puppy go potty indoors during the day. Here's how it works:

- ✔ Confine your puppy to the kitchen with some baby gates or an exercise pen and spread several layers of newspaper on the floor. Don't follow the indoor-training tips in Chapter 7 — you want to focus your actual training efforts on the outside.

- ✔ When you're home, pick up the papers and take him outside to do any and all bathroom business.

- ✔ Count the days till he reaches that 5-month mark. At that point, the papers are likely to stay dry all day. When that happens every day for at least a week, you can call a halt to the daytime papers: He's shown he can hold it all day.

Another situation that requires temporary indoor training is if your little darling is less than 4 months old, hasn't gotten all his shots, and has no outdoor place to potty except for the communal latrine (such as a park) that all the other dogs in the neighborhood use. Young puppies can easily get life-threatening diseases such as distemper and parvovirus (just ask Oprah Winfrey, who lost a puppy to parvo in 2009 and almost lost a second one) when they come into contact with the poop, pee, and/or vomit that infected dogs leave behind. A series of shots protects puppies from these diseases, but the shots aren't fully effective until the series is completed. That happens when the puppy is about 16 weeks old.

If you're a new-puppy owner who lives in the city, where the only outdoor potty spots are where other dogs do their business, heed your veterinarian's warnings. Let your canine baby potty indoors until he finishes his shots. After that, you can move his bathroom outside. For the lowdown on moving an indoor potty outside, see the next chapter.

Chapter 7

Making Some Inside Moves: Indoor Housetraining

*I*ndoor housetraining can benefit both people and pooches. The dog who potties inside need never worry about having to do his business outside in the rain, snow, and darkness. Indoor training can also save your floors and furnishings if your dog can't potty outdoors due to health reasons, your schedule, or your pup's tiny bladder.

In this chapter, I explain why indoor training can solve many pooches' potty problems, and I describe how to teach your canine companion to use an indoor potty.

Understanding How Indoor Training Works

Indoor training is the process of teaching your dog to poop and pee only in the indoor potty that you've created for him. Indoor training involves using scent and repetition to teach your dog that the indoor potty is the only surface upon which he should take a whiz or make a deposit. A successfully indoor-trained pooch is one who, upon feeling the urge to eliminate, high-tails himself to his indoor potty. When he's there, he does his business. Afterward, you clean the potty area.

Crates and the indoor trainee

If you're planning to indoor-train your puppy, does he really need a crate? Maybe not, but using one is still a good idea.

Every dog has an instinctive need for a safe, enclosed place from which to view the world: a den. A crate gives your dog that secure vantage point. Moreover, you probably don't want your dog to be traipsing to the papers or litter box at any and all hours. By teaching him to stay in his crate for at least fairly short intervals, you're helping him develop the control he needs to put a temporary hold on his deposits.

Of course, the devil is in the details, but take heart: You and your dog can master those details quickly and make indoor training a breeze. In this section, I help you recognize whether your dog is a good candidate for indoor training, and I discuss the importance of not confusing your dog with both indoor and outdoor potty places.

Identifying good indoor-training candidates

Picture this: A 2-year-old miniature Dachshund who was once a housetraining whiz suddenly appears to develop housetraining amnesia. He's always held his poop and pee all day, but when his owner starts working longer hours, his bathroom manners backslide, resulting in puddles all over his home. The owner, who's understandably frustrated at having to spend her evenings cleaning her carpet, wonders whether her dog needs a new way to go to the bathroom — and if so, whether indoor training would fill the bill. The answer to that question may be yes.

 Dealing with housetraining lapses should start with a trip to your vet. If your outdoor-trained dog suddenly starts making bathroom mistakes, have his vet examine him for possible medical problems (Chapter 10 outlines some of these problems and how to solve them.) But if your dog gets the all-clear from his doctor, switching to indoor training may be a good idea so that he can potty indoors whenever he needs to.

The following dogs may do better with indoor potties than with outdoor bathrooms:

> ✔ **Dogs who are home alone all day, especially puppies:** If you're away from home all day, moving the canine potty

indoors may be a big improvement from cleaning up a puddle when you come home. A puppy who's less than 4 or 5 months old can't hold it very long.

✔ **Pooches whose people have trouble walking:** For a senior citizen who can't get around easily, an indoor potty may make the difference between being able to have a dog and having to live without canine company.

✔ **Dogs who live in city apartments and can't get to an outdoor potty area easily:** For the high-rise apartment dweller, having an inside place for the dog to do his business can be far better than making a mad dash for the elevator to get Fido outside in time. However, this condition should apply to small dogs only.

✔ **Very small dogs:** For anyone with a reasonably small dog, indoor training eliminates the need to brave bad weather to take the dog to do the doo.

✔ **Puppies who can't use a public bathroom because they haven't finished their shots:** The bodily waste and vomit that other dogs leave behind can transmit devastating diseases such as canine distemper and parvovirus. So if your puppy hasn't been fully vaccinated — at about 16 weeks of age — and your dog has nowhere to go outside but a public park or similar area that other dogs visit, your pup may need to use an indoor potty, at least temporarily. (*Note:* If you have your own fenced backyard, letting him do his business outdoors is fine as long as you're reasonably sure that unvaccinated dogs haven't done their business there.)

Opting for indoor training only

You can train an outdoor-trained dog to use an indoor potty, and you can train an indoor-trained dog to do the doo outside. (For details, see the later sections "Switching a vaccinated puppy to outdoor training" and "Using Indoor Training for the Adult Dog.") But your dog shouldn't use both types of potty places on a regular basis. After you switch your dog's potty spot, close the old one.

You have to decide whether you want your dog to do his business inside or outside — and train him accordingly. It would be nice to be able to take your dog to an outdoor potty on sunny days but have the option of spreading out some newspapers when the weather's lousy or you feel like sleeping late. Unfortunately, though, this convenience for you just confuses your dog — and a dog who's confused about bathroom protocol is anything but convenient.

If your ultimate goal is to have your dog relieve himself outside, focus on outdoor training from the start. You can cover the puppy's indoor living area with papers to protect your floors (as I explain later in "Newspapers") if you'll be away from home for several hours and can't arrange for Fido to have a potty break. But don't pre-scent the papers with urine or praise the dog for doing the doo inside, as you would if you were specifically practicing indoor training. In this case, the newspapers are strictly a stop-gap measure until the puppy has the physical ability to hold it all day. See Chapter 11 for details on this technique.

Pick Your Potty: Deciding Which Type to Use

First, you need to decide which type of indoor potty to use: newspapers, puppy training pads, a litter box, or a grate/tray pooch potty. In this section, I describe your options and help you choose the one that may work best for you and your canine companion.

If you have a tiny dog, you may eventually want to put a potty on each floor of your home so she can reach the bathroom in time (see Chapter 9 for tips on working with petite pooches). Start with just one potty in the beginning for a puppy or adult housetrainee, because your dog will be confined much of the time. After housetraining is complete, you can add more doggie bathrooms.

Newspapers

Many people consider newspapers to be a temporary measure; they use the newspapers as a stop-gap doggie bathroom until the dog is ready to start doing her business outside on a full-time basis. That said, there's no reason newspapers can't be a permanent indoor potty for your pooch.

Newspapers are the original indoor pooch potties. And no wonder: They're cheap, they're readily available, and they can even be considered environmentally friendly: You buy one, you read it, and you reuse it as an indoor doggie bathroom. What could be simpler?

The drawbacks of papers are apparent the first time you clean up the poop or pee your dog places on that newspaper. Unless you pick up that paper with care, the pee may drip down onto the floor — or even (yuck) onto your person. There's also the not-so-attractive possibility that your dog will walk through her previous puddle or pile on subsequent trips to her newspaper potty if you don't clean up the mess right away. Still, for the cost-conscious, no-nonsense housetrainer who wants his pooch to perform her bathroom maneuvers indoors, newspapers can work.

Using newspapers is not just a matter of pulling out a sheet, throwing it on the floor, and letting your housetrainee figure out the rest. Here's how to construct a proper indoor bathroom:

- ✔ **Protect your floor.** Place an old shower curtain on the floor before you place any newspapers on it. The curtain protects your floor if the urine soaks through the papers. In that case, you only have to apply pet stain cleaner to the wet area of the curtain and wipe it dry.

- ✔ **Start big.** When you first lay out newspapers for your housetrainee, plan on covering an area equal to the size of at least four spread-out pages, one next to the other, if not nearly the dog's entire living area. That gives your pooch plenty of area upon which to potty when she's first figuring out where she's supposed to do her business.

- ✔ **Layer up.** Plan on using eight full-page spreads for your beginning housetrainee's newspaper bathroom area. Put four of those spreads together; then place the other four spreads next to the first set of spreads.

- ✔ **Shrink later.** As your dog becomes more proficient at using the papers, you can cut back on the number of papers used to just one four-layer set of two-page spreads.

- ✔ **Use the right newspaper.** Stick with newspapers that sport black print and occasional front page color photos. They're more absorbent than other surfaces, such as the Sunday ad inserts, and they provide more traction.

Don't fret if the ink from the newspaper rubs off on your light-coated puppy's paws. A little dab of soap and water can whisk those smudges away.

Puppy training pads

Puppy training pads, also known as *pee pads* or *pee-pee pads,* are marketed as an alternative to newspapers or litter boxes for dogs who are learning to potty indoors. The pads are made of absorbent layers of paper that are backed by a layer of plastic and are sealed around the edges. The standard size of each pad is 23 x 24 inches, although at least one manufacturer also offers an "oversize" pad of 30 x 30 inches. The pads come in packages usually ranging from 12 to 60 pads each.

Because the pads are absorbent, a puddle is less likely to soak through the floor than is the case with layers of newspaper, and cleanup is easier, too. However, I'm not a big fan of training pads.

All too often, dogs decide they'd rather eat puppy training pads than potty on them. At best, such ingestion results in a double mess on the floor: canine waste and shredded pads. At worst, a dog who eats his training pad may need emergency surgery to remove an ingested part of a pad that's blocked the digestive tract.

Litter boxes

Up until about a decade ago, newspapers were the main source of indoor potties for pooches. Then a couple of forward-thinking companies apparently realized that if cats could potty in aesthetically pleasing, easy-to-clean facilities, so could dogs. *Voilà* — the doggie litter box was born.

Litter boxes can offer other advantages: Unlike newspapers, they control pet waste odors and protect your floor without your having to sacrifice a shower curtain to the cause.

If you want to use a doggie litter box for training, you need the following items:

- ✔ **A litter box (also called a litter tray or litter pan), similar to what cats and kittens use to go to the bathroom:** The boxes have walls on three sides, and the fourth side is open to allow easy entry. One company, Nestlé-Purina, offers three litter box sizes: one for puppies and toy dogs, one for miniature-sized dogs, and one for standard-sized dogs that weigh up to 35 pounds.

- ✔ **The litter itself:** The main ingredients of dog litter are recycled paper and/or wood pulp. Costs vary depending on how large your dog is and what size of bag you purchase. You can also get dog litter delivered to your home if you order online or from a catalog.

Grate/tray potties

If you don't want to deal with the messiness of newspapers (including the chance that your dog will walk through the pee or poop deposited on those papers) or to add periodic purchases of dog litter to your pet care budget, you have yet another option: the grate/tray combo. These relatively new pooch potties come in two parts: an easy-to-clean plastic tray and a plastic grate that you place atop the tray. You don't need to buy anything else.

Avoiding kitty litter

If you have both a dog and a cat, you may be thinking about streamlining your shopping by purchasing the same litter for both. But according to litter manufacturers, that's not a very good idea.

For one thing, many dogs are as likely to try eating kitty litter as they are to eliminate in it. Such behavior can pose problems not only for your canine companion but also for your feline friend.

Moreover, kitty litter isn't designed to absorb doggie waste. Many cat litters, particularly the clumping kind, are sandlike in texture. Cats like to cover their solid waste, and the sandlike litter makes that cover-up action easier. Dogs don't cover their tracks — or their poop, either — but some canines do scuff and scrape the areas behind them with their rear feet after they've made a solid waste deposit. A dog who likes to do this would end up kicking a fair amount of kitty litter out of the box. Dog litters, which are made from recycled paper and/or wood pulp, are much more likely to withstand a dog's rear-guard action.

These differences in feline and canine behavior also mean that household dogs and cats need to have separate litter boxes. If you expect Fido to potty in the same box that Fluffy does — or vice versa — it's likely that both Fido and Fluffy will choose to do their business elsewhere.

And fear not: Because the grates are made of flexible plastic, they give under the weight of the dog's paws, preventing any discomfort. When I tested one of these combos with my 70-pound dog Allie, she didn't hesitate to venture onto the tray or to sit on it when asked.

But although grate/tray potties are just as nice looking as litter boxes, they can be cumbersome to clean up, depending on their size. That clumsiness of cleanup is also a reason not to use these potties for dogs who weigh more than 30 pounds.

Introducing Puppies to Indoor Training

The great thing about outdoor training is that you can start doing it right away. And if you're really lucky, your puppy's breeder has started the process for you. In this section, you find out how to show your dog his potty spot, how to encourage your dog with verbal cues, and how to develop a pup-sized training schedule.

Sod potties: Bringing the yard indoors

For apartment dwellers who still want their dogs to have the experience of pottying on grass (or a reasonable facsimile thereof), there's a new solution: Sod potties. These systems consist of a drain pan on which you place some real or faux sod. Some have their own drainage systems and even sprinklers (whoa!), and others require the owner to rinse the grass themselves, either by hand or with a hose.

These products have a certain ingenuity, but there's one huge drawback: cost. The least-expensive offering in this line of product starts at $199 — and that's not including the synthetic grass that you have to purchase. One top-of-the-line system that at least comes with its own grass costs nearly $600 to start with, not counting shipping costs. My opinion: Stick with the basics, unless you have money to burn.

Deciding where to put the indoor potty

Chapter 3 contains some basic pointers on where to put the indoor potty, mainly to help you make that decision. Now that you're tackling the nitty-gritty of indoor training, I offer more help not only on creating your pooch's indoor potty but also on setting up his entire living area. Accomplishing this task effectively can make bathroom breaks go much more smoothly for both you and your canine companion.

Until your dog is fully housetrained, he should not have access to your entire home unless you can be right there to watch his every move. If you don't watch what your four-legged friend is doing, you won't see when he performs a doggie download — and you'll miss what educators call a *teachable moment:* the opportunity to teach your canine companion where he should do his business.

But of course, no one can watch a dog 24/7. That's why, during the times you can't cast an eagle eye on your canine companion, you should confine him to a dog-proofed indoor living area. Start with a soft comfy bed — ideally inside a crate — and also set up a place for him to eat and a place for him to perform bathroom maneuvers.

When deciding where to set up your indoor trainee's living area, bear the following factors in mind:

- **Where the action is:** Your dog needs more than just a place to snooze, chow down, and do his bathroom biz. He also needs that living area to be where he's most likely to get attention from his family; in other words, where his family tends to congregate. For most households, that's the kitchen.

- ✔ **Surface stability:** No matter which indoor potty you choose, placement of that potty on a carpet will render the potty less stable than placement on a bare floor. Plus, if you choose to use newspapers, a big puddle of urine or pile of loose stool could soak through those newspapers onto the carpet, necessitating a challenging cleanup even though your dog went in the right place. For that reason, placing the living area on a bare floor is preferable to placing it on a carpet or rug.

- ✔ **Convenient waste disposal:** You may want to place the potty in a room close to a covered trash disposal area, a sink, and a toilet. That way, you can throw solid waste down the toilet, clean the potty itself in the sink if needed, and throw litter or papers in the trash area.

- ✔ **Your home décor:** If you've decorated your home to resemble an interior spread from *Architectural Digest*, you want to make sure that your puppy's part of your palace doesn't detract from your décor.

No matter where you place the living area, make sure that your puppy can't get into any trouble. Install baby gates to block the doorways, or encircle the living area with an exercise pen.

Within the living area, remove any dangling electrical cords from the dog's reach, and make sure he can't get into any cabinets where you keep cleaners and other hazardous substances. Door guards, which you can find in the baby departments of toy stores, can keep your curious canine from venturing into your cabinets.

Now you're ready to place the indoor potty in the living area. If you're using a litter box or grate/tray, place it in a corner away from your puppy's bed and dishes. If you're using newspapers, start by covering nearly the entire living area with four layers of newspaper. As your puppy develops potty proficiency, gradually reduce the coverage area.

Starting out

After you've set up your puppy's living area, you can start teaching her to use the indoor potty. The first and most important step is to help her make the connection between the potty place and what she's supposed to do in that place. In this section, I explain how it works.

Introducing the indoor potty

Start off right — and do it right away. The car ride home from the breeder, shelter, or foster home often prompts a puppy to eliminate immediately after the ride is over. So as soon as you and your pup arrive home, take her to her indoor potty. If she hesitates to use the potty, lure her onto it or into it with a small treat. When she opens her floodgates and/or makes a solid deposit, praise her lavishly and give her a tiny treat. If she doesn't do anything, wait a few minutes and then try again.

Cleaning up the indoor potty — mostly

Clean up the potty immediately, but leave a little something behind: a soiled newspaper or a scent cloth that you create by wiping your dog's bottom with a paper towel after she does the doo. Place this item just below the top layer of fresh newspaper or underneath the litter or grate. By doing so, you're telling your puppy where you want her to do her business. The smell of the soiled paper or litter is the canine equivalent of a come-hither glance.

Make sure that the puppy's potty spot remains sanitary. Here's how to keep it clean:

- **Newspapers:** Change the papers as soon as they're soiled (except for that pre-scented piece). If urine soaks through the papers to the shower curtain underneath it, just apply your pet stain cleaner to the dampened area and wipe it clean.

- **Litter box:** Plan on washing out the litter box with detergent and warm water at least once a week and on freshening the litter each time your dog uses the box.

- **Grate/tray indoor potty:** Rinse the grate and tray daily and wash them weekly unless the manufacturer's instructions dictate otherwise.

Taking later trips to the potty spot

After your dog has pottied and you've cleaned the potty, let your puppy explore the house for a while. But keep a close eye on her for signs that she needs to go again. If she suddenly stops, starts sniffing intently, begins to circle or pace, and/or starts to squat, whisk her back to the potty and praise her if she pees or poops there. Give her a tiny treat, too.

If you miss the signs that she's going to go and she has an accident, don't say anything. Just clean up and watch her more closely next time.

After an hour or so of getting to know each other, put your puppy in her bed (or crate) and let her take a much-needed nap. Watch to see when she wakes up, though — and when she does, get her to her potty. If she uses it, praise and treat. Then clean up as before.

Puppies need to potty after every meal, naptime, and play session. Each time she uses her potty, praise her lavishly.

Don't take your puppy outside for a walk or to play until after she makes a trip to the papers, box, or grate-tray combo. You don't want the pup to associate the outdoors with elimination. You're aiming to have your puppy consider the indoor potty her one and only toilet.

Scheduling bathroom breaks

Even indoor-trained dogs can benefit from learning to hold their poop and pee. The pooch with some self-control is much easier to live with than the dog with unregulated bathroom demands. Noticing that your dog may be ill is also easier if you can determine whether he's going more or less often than usual.

But regulating your dog's bathroom behavior needn't flummox you. You can bring some order to your indoor trainee's life (and your own) by putting his trips to the potty on a schedule.

The important thing to remember when setting up a potty schedule is that puppies need to eliminate at the following times:

- ✔ First thing in the morning
- ✔ Last thing at night
- ✔ During the night (if the puppy is under 4 months of age)
- ✔ After energetic playing
- ✔ After being confined in a crate
- ✔ After a nap
- ✔ After chewing on a toy or a bone
- ✔ A few minutes after eating

Armed with this knowledge, you can create a schedule that gives your puppy time to pee or poop and gives you some predictability. Table 7-1 shows how you can structure a schedule for a 3-month-old pup. Note, however, that a younger puppy probably will need to go much more often — maybe even hourly. (*Note:* This schedule assumes that someone's home during the day to take care of the puppy's potty needs. If that's not the situation in your home, check out Chapter 11.)

Table 7-1	Indoor Training Schedule for a 3-Month-Old Puppy
Time	*Tasks*
7:00 a.m.	Take puppy to potty. Feed puppy. Offer water. Take puppy to potty. Play with puppy up to 15 minutes. Take puppy to potty. Put puppy in crate.
Midmorning	Take puppy to potty. Offer water. Play with puppy up to 15 minutes. Take puppy to potty. Put puppy in crate.
Noon	Take puppy to potty. Feed puppy. Offer water. Take puppy to potty. Play with puppy 15 to 30 minutes. Take puppy to potty. Put puppy in crate.
Midafternoon	Take puppy to potty. Offer water. Play with puppy up to 15 minutes. Take puppy to potty. Put puppy in crate.
5:30 p.m.	Take puppy to potty. Feed puppy. Offer water. Take puppy to potty. Play with puppy up to 1 hour and/or let puppy hang out with the family in the kitchen.
7:00 p.m.	Take puppy to potty. Play with puppy up to 15 minutes. Put puppy in crate.
Before bed	Take puppy to potty. Put puppy in crate.
During the night	Take puppy to potty if necessary.

As your puppy gets older, she won't need the midmorning, midafternoon, and 7:00 p.m. trips to the potty, and she won't need the noontime feeding, either. The nocturnal trip to the potty will soon become a thing of the past, too.

Switching a vaccinated puppy to outdoor training

Maybe you never intended for indoor training to be a permanent solution. If you opted for indoor training because your pup wasn't fully vaccinated or because she was too young to hold it for very long, you can move the potty spot outdoors when the time is right. After the shots are finished at around 16 weeks of age, you can keep your puppy on papers if she's likely to be a small adult, or you can opt to move her bathroom outside.

If you want your puppy to go outside, start by moving the papers themselves to an outdoor area and let your puppy eliminate on them. Gradually reduce the size of the paper until the puppy just goes to her potty spot and does her business without paper.

Using Indoor Training for the Adult Dog

If you've just adopted an adult dog who's always pottied indoors, there's really no training to do. Just use the same type of bathroom he had in his previous home and continue with that. He'll probably adjust very smoothly with little or no effort on your part. If you don't know what type of indoor bathroom he had, choose what works best for you, set up a living area, and begin indoor training. (Chapter 6 includes a training schedule for adult dogs.)

More often, though, indoor training an adult dog means moving his bathroom from the outdoor backyard to a location inside your house. In this section, I give you the scoop on making that change, regardless of what kind of potty you've chosen.

As with indoor potties for puppies, you need to keep the potties for adult dogs sanitary. See the earlier section titled "Cleaning up the indoor potty — mostly" for details.

From outdoors to papers

Moving a dog's potty from an outdoor spot to the front page of yesterday's newspaper is relatively easy:

1. **Mark a piece of newspaper with your dog's urine.**

   Start by bringing a piece of toilet tissue and a piece of newspaper along when you take Fifi outdoors to her usual potty place. Wipe her bottom with the toilet tissue after she pees. Then wipe the toilet tissue onto the newspaper.

2. **Line your dog's outdoor potty spot with newspapers.**

   The next time you take Fifi out, take the pre-scented newspaper and some fresh newspaper along with you. When you reach the outdoor potty area, place the pre-scented paper on the ground and the fresh papers on top of it. Then let Fifi do her business atop the papers; praise and treat when she does. Continue this routine until Fifi uses the outdoor papers consistently.

3. **Move the papers indoors.**

   Place a pre-scented newspaper beneath the top layer of fresh newspapers spread out on the floor in the potty area you've chosen. Make sure that the area you cover equals two or three side-by-side two-page newspaper spreads and that it's four layers deep.

   At Fifi's next potty break, take her to the papers instead of outside. Give her a few minutes to do her business. If she does, praise lavishly; if she doesn't, wait 15 or 20 minutes and try again.

4. **When she consistently uses the indoor papers, reduce the amount of floor space the papers take up.**

Patience and encouragement are the keys to making this transition work. You're asking your dog to make a big change after years of doing her bathroom business outside. Dogs don't like changes any more than most people do, but your enthusiasm and her eagerness to please you can help her overcome her reluctance.

From outdoors to litter box

To help a dog switch from pottying outdoors to pottying in a litter box, start by bringing the new potty to the old potty. Here's how the process works:

1. **Just before one of your dog's scheduled bathroom breaks, put a little dog litter on his outdoor potty spot.**

Bring him to the outdoor spot and encourage him to do his business. Praise and treat him when he does.

2. **When he's consistently using the litter-covered outdoor potty, introduce him to the litter box.**

   Line the box with litter and place it next to the litter-covered outdoor potty area. Encourage him to investigate the litter box and praise him lavishly when he does.

3. **After your dog is used to seeing the litter box in his out-door potty area, introduce him to the idea of doing his business *inside* the box.**

   Put some used litter or pre-scented paper in the box. When he does eliminate inside the box, praise him and give him a treat.

4. **Start moving the litter box toward your house.**

   Do so just a short distance each day. Eventually, you'll be able to locate the litter box inside your home — and your days and nights of taking your dog outside to potty will be history.

If your dog balks at using the litter box at any point in this process, ease the pace of change. Make sure that he's mastered one step in the process before moving to the next one.

From outdoors to grate/tray combo

Here's how to train your outdoor-trained adult dog to use a grate/tray combo:

1. **Start by having your dog go potty outside; wipe your dog's bottom with a paper towel.**

   Hold onto this cloth; you'll use it to lure her to what will be her indoor potty.

2. **Sometime before the next potty break, break out the grate/tray combo indoors and use a treat to lure your dog atop the grate; keep doing this until she's walking on the grate comfortably.**

   Give her a treat when she does so. Keep doing this until she's comfortable atop the grate.

3. **For her next potty break, bring the grate/tray outside, place it next to her potty spot, and put the pre-scented cloth between the grate and tray.**

   If she goes on the grate and tray, praise and treat her.

4. **After she's done this a few times, start moving the potty toward your home at a snail's pace.**

The grate/tray combo eventually makes its way inside.

Responding to Mistakes

Your puppy or dog undoubtedly is wonderful, but he isn't perfect. Inevitably, he'll deposit a puddle or pile away from the indoor potty. But take a deep breath. Repeat to yourself, "It's not his fault. It's not his fault." Take him to his indoor living area and say nothing. Then go get some paper towels and pet stain remover. Clean up according to the directions on the cleaner.

Above all, don't scold, punish, or try to correct your dog. He won't connect your loud voice and angry gestures with the fact that he went to the bathroom a mere ten minutes ago.

If your dog folds back his ears and puts his tail between his legs while you let him know how upset you are, don't think — not for a minute — that he's feeling guilty. He's apprehensive, upset, maybe even fearful when you become angry, but he feels absolutely no remorse over doing what came naturally to him. So don't waste your breath; just clean up the mess.

Then ask yourself what you could've done to prevent your dog's accident. Table 7-2 can help get you started.

Table 7-2	Troubleshooting Fido's Accident
What Fido Did	*What You Should Do*
He peed when you weren't looking.	Don't let him out of his living area unless you can watch him every single second.
He pooped without warning.	Watch to see how he acts or what he does right before he unloads. That way, you'll be able to whisk him to his indoor potty before he has an accident.
He missed the potty.	Leave him a bigger area of newspapers for him to eliminate on, or get him a bigger litter box or grate/tray combo.
He pees on the same spot.	Clean up completely (see Chapter 3 for details).

Chapter 8

Fine-Tuning Housetraining

- -

- -

*P*lenty of signs can indicate that a dog has mastered
Housetraining 101. Here are a few:

✔ You haven't used your commercial pet stain cleaner for
weeks, whereas a month or so ago you were using it almost
every day. An unused bottle of cleaner probably means that
your puppy pal isn't having any indoor accidents.

✔ You're consistently scooping up litter or cleaning up either
soiled papers or a bathroom tray soon after each meal you
serve your indoor-trained dog. This after-dinner (or after-
breakfast) ritual means that your four-legged friend is eliminating on a regular schedule and probably isn't having any
out-of-potty accidents.

✔ You come home from work and find that the newspapers that
you left for your dog in the morning are unsullied by canine
poop or pee. Moreover, the papers have consistently gone
unused over the past couple of weeks. Consistently clean
papers signal that your canine companion is holding his poop
and pee all day and is confining his bathroom maneuvers to
outdoor turf.

If your dog shows these or similar signs of housetraining mastery,
congratulations to both of you on a job well done! By successfully
teaching your dog basic bathroom manners, the two of you have
laid the foundation for a rich and rewarding friendship.

But why stop there? Maybe your dog can learn to ask to go out if he
isn't doing so already. And life certainly would be easier if your dog
were to master the ultimate housetraining feat: doing his business
as soon as you tell him to. Think what it'd be like to be able to take

your dog out at night and not have to walk up and down your block until he decided to pee. Instead, you could march him to a particular potty spot, tell him something like "Fido, do your business!" and know that Fido would do just that. This chapter helps you teach him these advanced bathroom maneuvers and more.

Decoding Pre-potty Maneuvers

Before you can boost your dog's housetraining skills to the advanced level, you need to decode his individual potty style. In other words, you need to know exactly what he does just before he actually eliminates.

Why is this knowledge so important? Because the key to teaching your dog advanced bathroom manners is being able to anticipate when he needs to take a whiz or make a deposit. Fortunately, most dogs provide clear signs that the urge to poop or pee is taking hold. The trick for you is to observe the signs that *your* dog exhibits. Then you can put your observations to work as you teach him those fancy bathroom maneuvers.

Here are a few common examples of pre-bathroom behavior. In general, the more intensely and purposefully the dog is performing his pre-potty maneuver, the more likely he is to actually poop or pee.

- ✔ **The Statue:** Some dogs simply call a halt to any and all activity and stand as still as statues. Seconds later, they start to do their business. This no-frills approach to elimination is very common among young puppies, who frequently don't realize that they need to go until they're just about to do the deed.

- ✔ **The Pacer:** Many pooches engage in back-and-forth pacing before they eliminate. When such a dog is near her potty spot, she begins to walk in one direction and then turns around and walks an equal distance in the opposite direction. Depending on how badly she needs to go, she may walk back and forth once or twice — or as many as a dozen times.

    Many a Pacer starts her pre-potty routine by walking as far as 5 or 6 feet in each direction. As the urge to go strengthens, she gradually shortens the pacing distance until she's trotting only a few inches back and forth. At that point, the dog eliminates. The speed at which a Pacer does her thing varies, although a speedy pace usually indicates that she'll be unloading momentarily.

- ✔ **The Circler:** Quite a few dogs start walking around in circles just before they eliminate. The sizes of these pre-potty circles vary: Some have diameters that aren't much bigger than the dogs themselves, and other circles may sport diameters of several feet. Speed varies, too, although just as with the Pacer, the faster the circling, the more imminent the potty event usually is. In fact, some Circlers literally run rings around their people just before pottying.

✔ **The Sniffer:** Almost every dog engages in some sort of pre-potty sniffing before he actually does the deed. Some dogs sniff before beginning to circle or pace; others confine their pre-potty maneuvers to intense snuffling of a particular spot just before peeing or pooping on it.

As with circling and pacing, a dog's sniffing speed varies greatly depending on how intense the urge to eliminate is. Generally, a dog who's moving his nose along the ground in a leisurely manner is still searching for what he considers to be a proper place to potty. However, intense, concentrated sniffing of a specific spot often indicates that a dog is about to anoint that spot.

✔ **The Beeliner:** Some dogs, such as my Golden Retriever, Allie, take a linear approach to finding a potty spot. They sniff a little bit but then make a beeline for the place where they want to poop or pee. If this description fits your dog and you're walking her on leash, be sure to hold tight to that leash after she starts sniffing.

✔ **The False Alarmist:** Some dogs are so particular about where they do their business that they engage repeatedly in one or more of the pre-potty maneuvers outlined in this list, only to stop before actually eliminating. Cory, my late, great Sheltie, was a master of this technique, and Allie is becoming a quick study. Still, you can decode such a dog's pre-potty behavior by paying a little closer attention to what happens when your dog actually does go. For example, most female dogs not only squat but also stretch out their backs before they pee. When Allie squats but fails to execute that pee-pee stretch, I know that she's changed her mind about anointing that particular spot.

Some dogs adopt more than one potty style throughout their lives and even within the same potty break. For example, Cory tended to be a Circler before he peed but was more of a Pacer before he pooped. Allie is a classic Sniffer but also is quite the Beeliner, especially when I bring her near a spot where she's done her business before or where she realizes other dogs have done their business prior to her arrival.

In any case, after you identify your own canine companion's potty style(s), you're ready to teach him some advanced bathroom manners, starting with asking to go out.

Getting Your Dog to Ask to Go Out

A great skill is for a dog to somehow communicate to her people that she needs a potty break. Some dogs, like my Sheltie Cory, teach themselves to ask their people to take them out (see the nearby "Cory becomes teacher's pet" sidebar). Others need a little help from their humans. If your dog falls into the latter category, this section's for you.

Sometimes all you need to do is put the leash in the same place every time you hang it up. That was true for Cory. My family and I always hung his leash on the same doorknob every time we came back inside from a trip to the potty. By always putting the leash in the same place and by always using the leash when we needed to take Cory out, our Sheltie guy soon figured out that the fastest way to tell us what he needed was to go to his leash and tap it with his nose. You can do the same thing when you housetrain your dog.

Put the leash in the same place each and every time. Use the same words whenever you take your canine companion to his outdoor potty spot. Do exactly the same thing every time you take your four-legged friend out, and you create the conditions that help him figure out a way to tell you when he needs to go.

But if you don't want to play a waiting game, don't hesitate to take a more active approach to teaching your dog to ask for a potty break. Here's what to do:

1. **Get a signal maker.**

   Find something that can hang from a doorknob within reach of your dog's nose or paw and also makes a pleasant noise when the dog touches it lightly. A set of Christmas bells fits the bill.

2. **Teach the signal.**

   Every time you take your dog out for a potty break, ring the bells. Do this consistently so that your canine companion associates the ringing of the bells with your taking her outside.

3. **Let her try.**

   Sooner or later, your dog will want to check out the bells herself. Encourage her to do so: Praise her enthusiastically if she even sniffs the bells.

4. Heed her signal.

The first time your dog taps the bells with her paw or nose (see Figure 8-1), respond promptly: Take her outside! Bring her to her potty spot and praise her lavishly if she goes. After a few times, your dog connects her ringing of the bells with your taking her outside.

Figure 8-1: Your dog doesn't have to say a word to tell you when she needs to go out.

Don't let your four-legged friend fool you. If your puppy rings the bells but fails to do her duty when she's outside, march her back inside.

Many dogs figure out their own ways to tell their people that it's potty time. For example, Allie employs one of two methods to tell me that the bathroom urge is upon her: coming over to me and staring at me or running into the family room and scratching on the door that leads outside. Just as you watch your dog to decode her potty style, study her behavior to see what she does to tell you that she needs a bathroom break. Her signals may be quite subtle, but if you pay close attention, you can probably see how she's trying to convey what she needs to do and what you need to know.

Cory becomes teacher's pet

For every dog who's the subject of a housetraining horror story, another dog quickly decodes the do's and don'ts of proper canine bathroom behavior. Fortunately for me, one of the latter dogs was my dearly departed Sheltie, Cory.

Of course, I want to believe that one of the factors behind Cory's housetraining prowess was the possibility that *I* was doing something right. But whatever the reasons were, my outdoor-trained Sheltie guy had only a couple of indoor potty accidents during his entire housetraining process.

The funny thing was that it took me a long time to realize how well Cory was doing. I followed the outdoor training schedule outlined in Chapter 6 until Cory was well beyond his 3-month birthday. After that, I gradually cut back on the amount of time he spent in his crate and increased the amount of time he could run around the house. But I watched him like a hawk the whole time; he didn't get any unsupervised time at all.

Then, one morning when Cory was about 6 months old, he surprised me. He and I were playing together, and although he wasn't due for a bathroom break, he suddenly stopped what he was doing. Then he walked over to the doorknob where his leash was hanging and tapped the leash with his nose before turning to stare at me.

I'm no rocket scientist, but I suspected that Cory was asking me to take him out. So I snapped on his leash and walked him outside to the median strip in front of our house. As soon as we reached the strip, Cory opened his floodgates. I was thrilled. And I figured that if Cory could tell me when he needed a bathroom break, I didn't have to worry about him having an accident in the house. In short, I was ready to consider him fully housetrained. And from that point on, Cory fully justified my faith in his bathroom abilities: He never relieved himself in our house for the rest of his life. He clearly had gotten the housetraining thing down pat.

Encouraging Elimination

Picture this: a dark and stormy night. You and your canine companion have spent a blissful couch-potato evening. Now it's almost bedtime, but instead of moving directly from sofa to bed you have one final task to accomplish: taking your dog out for his last potty break of the day. And you're dreading it.

During most weather, you don't mind the end-of-the-day trip outside to your dog's potty spot. On nights like this one, though, the p.m. pit stop is quite another matter. Like most dogs, your special friend dislikes doing his business in the rain. Add some wind and cold, and the dislike mushrooms into out-and-out hatred. At such times, you just know that when you let him out to do his business, he'll stand next to the door, shiver, and attempt to look pitiful. Under no circumstances will he allow the damp ground to even brush against his hindquarters. And no way will he actually unload in the rain.

Having you with him doesn't spur your pee- or poop-retentive pooch, either. What happens instead is that the two of you get to stand outside and get soaked together. That's not my idea of quality time, and it's probably not yours, either.

Some lucky owners are able to teach their dogs to do their business on cue. Others, me included, have dogs who set their own potty agendas, thank you very much. That said, you can still encourage such dogs to potty sooner rather than later. Here, I discuss how to teach your dog to unload when you ask him to and how to cope if your dog replies, in effect, "I'll go when I decide to go."

Peeing on cue

The theory behind the peeing-on-cue maneuver is simple: You help your dog associate a kind of potty prompt with the act of urinating. When your dog makes that connection, he'll pee when you ask him to. Thus, when you and Fido are out in the rain, you simply march together to the potty spot, you cue Fido to pee, and *voilà!* He does.

In fact, your newly housetrained puppy may already pee when you ask him to if you've followed the instructions for outdoor training in Chapter 6. But even if your four-legged friend hasn't mastered this maneuver, you can still teach even an adult dog with fully entrenched bathroom habits to do his business when you ask him to. Here's how:

1. **Pick a potty prompt.**

   Make this decision carefully. The ideal bathroom command is a phrase that you can use without embarrassment. For example, you may feel more comfortable telling your dog, "Fido, do your business," rather than "Fido, go take a leak."

   Be careful that the prompt is a phrase that you'll use *only* when telling Fido to pee. A more general-sounding prompt, such as "Hurry up," can bring unwelcome results, such as Fido's anointing the carpet at the same time you're telling your children to get out the door so that they won't be late for school.

2. **Take your dog to his potty spot the next time he has to do his bathroom business.**

3. **Watch for pre-potty signals.**

   If you've taken the time to acquaint yourself with his potty style, you know what to look for (see the earlier section "Decoding Pre-potty Maneuvers"). When he starts those maneuvers, get ready to see him pee.

4. **Give the prompt as soon as your dog starts to pee.**

5. **Praise him lavishly and give him a small treat when he's finished.**

Within a couple of weeks, he'll likely have made the connection between the potty prompt and the act of urinating and respond accordingly.

Prompting Mr. (or Ms.) Independent

I have a confession to make: Although I'm familiar with the mechanics of teaching a dog to urinate on cue, my own canine companions just won't do it.

Some of my friends tease me about my Golden Retriever Allie's (or before her arrival, Cory the Sheltie's) refusal to learn this maneuver. They want to know how I can possibly write a book about housetraining if I can't even get my own dog to piddle when prompted. (In my defense, their lack of motivation probably isn't my fault; see the nearby sidebar for details.)

To make matters worse, some dogs' pre-potty behavior is, to put it mildly, erratic. Cory sometimes offered no warning at all that he was about to eliminate outdoors. He'd just be walking along when suddenly he'd stop and do the deed before I even realized what was going on. Other times, he'd pull so many false alarms that I gave up trying to anticipate when he'd actually go. Allie, my present canine companion, has also mastered the dubious art of the false alarm, going so far as to actually squat and then stand up and begin moving again without having unloaded anything. Consequently, I've had a hard time teaching each dog to potty on cue, because they offered conflicting information about when they were really going to go.

But even if your dog defies your efforts to teach him a potty prompt, you can still speed up his pee-pee process. Here's how:

✔ **Fake him out.** So what if it's raining? If you act as if walking in a downpour is more fun than playing fetch, your dog may believe you — and that belief may help him relax enough to go.

✔ **Stay loose.** A dog is more likely to do his business if he's relaxed rather than tense. For that reason, be sure to stay relaxed, calm, and happy when you take your dog out for a potty break. If you feel yourself tensing up because your dog won't go, take him back inside and try again in a few minutes when you're both more relaxed.

✔ **Praise him before the fact.** If your dog shows the slightest hint that he's going to go — for me, it's when Allie moves from the sidewalk to the grass of the median strip — praise him lavishly. By doing so, you may help him realize that he's got the right idea and encourage him to follow through.

✔ **Find a familiar spot.** Often, you can jump-start your dog's urge to pee by taking him to the spot he anointed on his previous trip out. Chances are he'll remember what he did there before and do it again.

✔ **Find a communal potty.** If you can't remember where your dog went during your previous trip outside, take him someplace where you know other dogs have pottied. The scent of previously deposited canine calling cards may prompt your dog to leave a card of his own.

Both Cory and Allie tended to employ a kind of Murphy's Law to their bad-weather bathroom maneuvers. At the times that I most wanted them to pee when I said to — such as late at night and/or during a downpour — my canine companions often decided to vie for the title of Mr. or Ms. Iron Bladder. Be it hail or snow, rain or sleet, when the weather was bad, Cory tended to shut his floodgates tight. If I got uptight or angry over this pee-pee retentive behavior, he made it clear that he thought any sort of walk was a bad idea. He'd actually try to pull me back into the house. Allie's not quite as sensitive as my Sheltie guy was, but her distaste for whizzing in bad weather, much less dumping, becomes quite clear when the rain is pouring or the wind is howling.

Deciding When to Grant More Freedom

The fact that your dog has become a housetraining ace doesn't necessarily mean that she's ready to have full run of your house. Many housetraining graduates still need to have their access to their homes restricted. The reasons such restrictions may be necessary basically boil down to two: Either your puppy isn't old enough to be considered truly housetrained, or she's not dependable enough to leave your stuff alone when she's left alone.

Here's my card: Leaving a message

In the "Encouraging Elimination" section, I lament my problems teaching my own dogs to go on cue. But experts note that I shouldn't consider my inability to teach a potty prompt to be a failure on my part or a lack of intelligence on the parts of my dogs Cory and Allie. Such dogs just may not be interested in learning to pee on cue. The reason: For such dogs, the act of urinating means a whole lot more than emptying their bladders.

Certain dogs actually value their urine. Such dogs sprinkle pee carefully onto only what they consider to be the very best surfaces — surfaces they've selected on the basis of size, prominence, and preexisting odors. For these canines, their pee is their calling card — their announcement at a local street corner that they've been at that corner. These dogs are much less likely to evacuate their bladders at times and places they haven't chosen than other, less exacting dogs are.

Such dogs also sniff the ground, the pole beneath the corner stop sign, and just about any other vertical object to determine whether other dogs have left *their* calling cards behind. A dog can tell a lot about another dog simply by sniffing a drop of that dog's pee. For example, one sniff of a local canine potty place can tell a romance-seeking male dog not only whether ladies have been in the area but also whether those ladies are in the mood for love (in other words, whether they're in heat).

The age factor: How old is old enough?

One issue you need to keep in mind when determining whether your little pooch is ready for more freedom is age. Even if your puppy shows signs of being a housetraining prodigy, think twice about declaring her fully housetrained if she's less than 6 months old.

A puppy under the age of 6 months may know when and where it's okay to potty, but she may not always be physically able to keep from occasionally anointing your carpet or making a deposit on your floor — especially if she doesn't have fairly frequent access to her designated bathroom.

So even if your precocious little darling hasn't had an accident in weeks, don't assume that she can hold it at any and all times. And don't push the outer edge of her potty endurance envelope. Continue to keep her confined when you can't supervise her until she at least passes her half-year birthday.

Even after you decide to loosen the reins a bit, give her only a little unsupervised freedom at a time. Just as you wouldn't let a newly licensed teenage driver attempt a cross-country trip immediately, you shouldn't let a newly housetrained puppy have immediate access to your entire house all day.

Confine your housetraining graduate to one or two rooms for a couple of hours or so and see how she does. Watch to see not only whether she holds her poop and pee but also whether she decides to dig or chew on any forbidden household objects. If she passes muster, gradually give her more freedom. But as with human children, don't give your dog too much freedom too soon.

The responsibility factor: Should she have freedom of the house?

Another point to consider when deciding to give your dog more roaming rights is dependability. Even if your dog or puppy has mastered the fine art of housetraining, that doesn't mean she should have total freedom of the house — at least not when you're out of the house. That depends on her maturity level and history of behavior when left alone.

Even if your housetraining ace knows not to do her business inside your domicile, she may indulge her desire to make other mischief in said domicile. Allie, my Golden Retriever, is a case in point. Even after she became a housetraining graduate, she would cause other problems, such as going into the garbage, scratching on the sofa (and pulling out the stuffing), chewing the TV remote, unwinding toilet paper, and shredding magazines within her reach, sometimes right under our very noses.

How do you determine whether your dog is ready to be left unsupervised in the house? You probably need to engage in a little trial and error. Try leaving her alone for brief periods of time and see how she does. Initially start at 5 minutes and gradually increase to up to 30 minutes. If she hasn't started wreaking havoc in 30 minutes, she's probably ready to spend alone time outside the crate. Even then, though, proceed cautiously and reduce temptation. Here's how:

✔ **Start slow.** Begin your dog's road to freedom by giving her access to only one or two rooms in the house while you're away. If she doesn't engage in destructive or otherwise undesirable behavior, you can gradually allow her to spend time in more rooms of the house.

✔ **Remove temptation.** Your dog's chances of handling her newly bestowed freedom successfully increase if you set her up for that success. So if you know she likes to chew up toilet paper, keep your bathroom door closed. If she's a champion counter-surfer, make sure no food's left out on your kitchen counter. If she likes to raid the garbage, block access to the garbage can. If laundry is her thing, keep the laundry room door closed and block her access to all clothes hampers. You get the idea.

✔ **Secure items before leaving.** At least in the initial stages of allowing your dog freedom of the house, take the time before you leave to make sure you haven't left any temptations for her.

My family and I quickly learned to reduce Allie's environmental temptations by closing bathroom doors, blocking off the garbage can with barstools and the sofa with dining chairs, and putting magazines and TV remotes beyond her reach. But for four years or so thereafter, we also crated Allie (using the nighty-night cue I describe in Chapter 5) whenever we left the house just to protect our stuff from the ravages of her paws and chompers. Only since she turned 5 and started showing some semblance of doggie dignity and respect for our possessions while we were in the house — and after she successfully dealt with short increments of freedom when we left the house — did we begin to allow her freedom of the house any time we went out, no matter how long we were gone. And she's done fine — notwithstanding the shredded magazine that I found on the floor after I got back from running errands this morning. But that was my bad: I should've put it out of her reach before I left.

Part III
Solving Housetraining Problems

The 5th Wave   By Rich Tennant

"Submissive urination, huh? That's something I tolerate in my managers, but not in my dog."

In this part...

Generally, housetraining proceeds pretty smoothly after you get the hang of it. Still, just as with any new endeavor, progress may take the form of going two steps forward, one step back. Here, you get the lowdown on how to deal effectively with the main reasons those backward steps occur: a dog's behavioral problems, a dog's health problems, and (alas!) problems caused by the humans in the household.

Chapter 9

Accident-Proofing Small Dogs and Other Problem Potty-ers

In This Chapter

▶ Describing dogs with bathroom issues

▶ Solving common canine potty problems

Almost every dog has housetraining problems at one time or another. Some pooches have trouble mastering their bathroom basics. Others ace Housetraining 101 but run into toilet trouble later. Whether your dog's potty problems make him a slow learner or conflicted canine, help is at hand. Among the following profiles of dogs with potty issues may be one that sheds light on your housetrainee's particular problem and how to solve it.

The Teensy-Weensy Tinkler

As a pet journalist, I've written my share of dog breed profiles for magazines and Web sites. One thing that's always struck me is that whenever I'm writing about a very small dog, such as a Chihuahua or Shih Tzu, the owners I interview invariably tell me that these pint-sized pooches have big-sized housetraining problems. Basically, I'm told, the little guys and gals wash out of basic housetraining.

However, experts disagree among themselves as to whether that's actually the case. Some do contend that very little dogs have some very big disadvantages when learning proper potty protocol. Here are some housetraining hurdles the experts suggest:

▶ **Bladder size:** Teensy-weensy dogs have teensy-weensy bladders that can't hold very much urine. That means small dogs have to discharge that urine a lot more often than their bigger counterparts need to — and a lot more often than their human owners may anticipate.

✔ **Sense of space:** Because they're so little, small dogs' sense of space differs from that of larger-sized dogs. For example, getting to an outdoor potty from inside the house may seem like a huge distance to a Chihuahua, whereas to a Golden Retriever, that same distance is just a hop, skip, and a jump away. Given such differences, the Chihuahua is less likely to reach his spot in time than the Golden is.

Other experts, though, contend that people, not pooches, are the reasons very small dogs can find housetraining more difficult. People who live with tiny tinklers may find these dogs so cute that they aren't as vigilant about housetraining as people who have larger dogs are. Compounding the problem is the fact that *les petits chiens* make much smaller puddles than their bigger brethren do. Consequently, those puddles are far easier to overlook than the larger ponds and lakes that emerge from bigger dogs — at least until the little dog reanoints that same spot a few times or does that reanointing in front of a guest. Then it's not okay — but it shouldn't have been okay in the first place.

No matter what side of the debate you come down on, though, you can help your little dog become a housetraining ace. This section explains how.

Choose the right potty place

A little dog needs a potty place that she can get to quickly — or that you can get her to quickly. If you choose to have her do her business indoors, make sure her indoor potty is accessible at all times. And you don't need to have just one such potty: Putting a litter box or other doggie toilet on each floor of your home can up the odds that your petite pooch will reach her spot in time. I discuss indoor training in Chapter 7.

If you'd rather have her do the doo outside, choose a potty spot that's close to your home or apartment building, and take her to this spot for any and all potty breaks. See Chapter 6 for more on outdoor training.

Don't push your luck (or her bladder)

Because your little dog's capacity to hold her water or other stuff is limited, she's more likely to respond to schedule changes with an unauthorized doggie offload. In other words, if you miss one of her scheduled bathroom breaks, you should count on having something to clean up later.

Be considerate of your teensy tinkler, particularly her teensy bladder. Simple logic seems to indicate that the little dog's bladder needs relieving more often than the bigger dog's larger bladder does. Either plan on either taking your small dog to her outdoor potty spot more often or opt for indoor training so she can get to an indoor bathroom all by herself.

Consistency helps your little dog develop her capacity to wait until she has a chance to potty in the proper place. For those reasons, setting up and sticking with a *reasonable* schedule is especially important when a housetraining student is big of heart but small in stature. I discuss setting up a schedule in Chapters 6 and 7.

Don't excuse lapses

No matter how big or little the pooch is, she shouldn't be allowed to pee or poop wherever she chooses. Canine bodily waste smells bad, stains carpets and floors, and contains bacteria that can make both dogs and people sick. Consequently, housetraining is just as important for little dogs as for big ones.

Don't let your pint-sized pooch's cuteness get in the way of teaching her bathroom basics. If she has an accident, deal with it the same way you deal with an accident by a larger dog: Figure out what went wrong (specifically, what you did wrong) and resolve not to let it happen again.

As with larger dogs, a crucial component to successfully housetraining a small dog is to remove any and all residue of toileting transgressions — and the odors from such transgressions, too. Use a good cleaner designed especially for pet stains to remove the evidence of unauthorized tinkles. Failure to clean up promptly and thoroughly will have the same result no matter what your dog's size is: She'll come back and repeat her performance upon the very same spot. Chapter 3 discusses suitable cleaners.

The Dog Who Pees Lying Down

When you come home, does your canine companion fold her ears back, look away from you, and tuck her wagging tail between her legs? If you bend over to put the leash on her, does she roll onto her back? And does she dribble a little bit of urine at such times — whether lying on her back or standing on all fours?

If so, take heart. Your dog doesn't have a housetraining problem at all. The urine she dribbles doesn't indicate a lack of bathroom manners. Instead, she's trying to tell you that she worships the ground you walk on.

Dogs who look away from a person or another canine, tuck their tails between their legs, fold back their ears, and leak a little bit of urine are showing what experts call *submissive behavior*. In other words, they're willing to yield to the wishes of the more dominant individual. The little puddle on the ground emphasizes this respect. And if the dog leaks this urine while lying on her back, she's being even more submissive. She is not making a housetraining mistake.

You need to treat the submissive dog very gently. She's a highly sensitive individual who needs your help to gain a little bit more self-confidence or at least time to collect herself so that she doesn't pee on your floor or carpet. Here are some ideas to help her — and to rescue your floors.

Play it cool

Ignore her. Yes, really. When you come home in the evening or at any other time after being away for a while, don't pay any attention to your ecstatic pooch, no matter how much she throws herself at you or tries to get your attention. By ignoring your submissive dog and giving her a few minutes to calm down, you reduce the likelihood that she'll dribble. After a few minutes, you should be able to say hello to her.

When you do greet your dog, whether you've just returned from the other room or a long day at work, don't make a big deal of it. Say a quiet hello, smile at her, and maybe give her a little pat. Don't hug her, smooch her, coo to her, or make any excited baby talk to her, no matter how happy you are to see her. Your objective here is to help her stay calm so that she doesn't pee.

And do extend your play-it-cool policy to visitors: Ask them to ignore your dog when they first enter your home. That way, she'll have time to collect herself and calm down before she greets your company.

Get down to her level

Some submissive dogs start leaking when their human leaders stand over them — for example, to put on their leashes. If yours is such a pooch, try squatting or sitting on the floor so that your eyes are level with your dog's.

By getting down to her level, you avoid giving your dog the message that you are the leader and she is not. That message is what prompts her to pee in response. In effect, she's saying, "I know you're the boss, and I'll do whatever you ask." Don't worry that your dog will decide to be Ms. Alpha if you try this technique. You can give your dog confidence without relinquishing your position and responsibility.

Don't stare her down

Some submissive dogs start dribbling when their special persons look directly into their eyes. That's because in dog-talk, a direct gaze or stare is considered a dominant, I'm-the-boss type of gesture — and a submissive dog will pee to show that she understands her lowly place in the family hierarchy. But if you look away, she won't need to make that submissive response.

The Dog Who Leaves His Mark

If you're seeing dribs and drabs of dog pee on vertical surfaces inside your home, your pooch probably doesn't have a housetraining problem. A more likely possibility is that he's dealing with turf or relationship issues.

Dogs pee not only because their bladders are full but also because they want to communicate with other canines. Just about any dog will sniff the place where another dog took a whiz, and often the sniffer will decide to pee on the same spot. However, an intact male dog may lift his leg and direct a little jet stream onto vertical surfaces so that he can announce that those surfaces are part of his domain. In other words, such a dog uses his pee to mark his territory.

Dealing successfully with the Dog Who Leaves His Mark requires several actions. Here's what you should do.

Neuter him

Your canine guy is likely to be less concerned about whose turf is whose if he's not at the mercy of his raging canine male hormones. By neutering him, you give him some welcome relief (no, not that kind of relief!).

Make sure that any other animals in the house also are spayed or neutered. Your local animal shelter or rescue group may be able to direct you to low-cost spaying and neutering services.

Building Molly's confidence

Years ago, I adopted a little mixed Poodle named Molly, who was a very submissive dog. Every day, she would greet my nightly homecomings by rolling onto her back and leaking urine onto my foyer floor.

To help Molly collect herself, I would restrain myself from petting her or even talking to her when I came home. Instead, I would silently sit on the floor and wait for her to come to me. When she reached me, I would look away from her and attach the leash to her collar. After several months of this routine, Molly finally felt sufficiently calm and confident to hold her water when I came home from work at night.

Remove (or at least contain) the target

Sometimes you can deal with canine target practices by eliminating the dog's access to the target. For example, if your dog likes to mark the chair in your partner's home office, keep the door to that office closed. If your four-legged friend likes to direct his efforts toward your Christmas tree, consider enclosing the tree in an *exercise pen,* which resembles a floorless child's playpen. I know someone who does just that; in fact, she even decorates the ex-pen so that it looks as though it was always meant to be part of her holiday décor. (For a description of ex-pens, check out Chapter 3.)

Remind him who's top dog

A dog who's engaging in marking behavior may need to be reminded who is the top dog in his household (and that should be you). As his benevolent leader, you should insist that he earn any privileges. Have him sit or ask him to do something else before you feed him, take him for a walk, start a play session, or do anything else that he enjoys.

If you haven't done so already, find an obedience class for yourself and your dog. By teaching him maneuvers such as coming when called, sitting, and lying down, you make it clear to your dog that you're the leader of his pack and that he has no need to tell you whose turf is whose.

Build a peaceable kingdom

Years ago, when I was staying at a friend's country home for the first time, I awoke in the middle of one night just in time to see my friend's dog lift his leg and anoint the corner of the bed I was sleeping in. The dog's message was clear: I was an interloper, and he didn't appreciate my presence.

If your dog is marking his turf because an unfamiliar human guest is in the house, show your canine companion that he has nothing to worry about. Have the guest play with or feed the dog. As soon as Fido realizes that the guest is a friend rather than a threat, the marking behavior may stop.

On the other hand, perhaps your dog is displaying his marksmanship to establish his place among the other four-legged members of your household. If that's the case, try to resolve any conflicts between the marker and your other pets. Feed them separately from each other — at different times and/or in different locations — and try to give each animal equal amounts of affection.

Start remedial housetraining

If your dog likes to mark his territory, set up a housetraining routine such as the ones in Chapters 6 and 7 and follow it religiously until your dog confines his peeing to the papers, litter box, grate/tray combo, or outdoors.

If you see your dog start to lift his leg and/or anoint a surface, distract him by clapping your hands or making some other loud noise. Then get him to his potty area pronto.

Also make sure that you thoroughly clean any area that your dog has anointed or pooped upon. Otherwise, the smell of the previous dousing will bring him to the same spot for an encore performance. Check out Chapter 3 for information on effective indoor cleaners.

Canine marking behavior can be difficult to, well, eliminate. If your dog persists in christening unauthorized areas, ask your vet for a referral to a qualified trainer, certified applied animal behaviorist, or veterinary behaviorist. The sidebar "Picking among experts" explains how these experts differ.

The Uptight Canine

Scientists are starting to realize that dogs experience at least some emotions that are very similar to those that humans experience. Among those emotions is anxiety. Yup, just as with people, certain situations cause certain dogs to get uptight — and some of those anxiety-ridden creatures end up having bathroom accidents.

Dogs are social creatures, so separation anxiety is one of the most common forms of anxiety in dogs. Although almost every dog relishes any and all opportunities to hang out with his people, some dogs really can't deal with being left alone. Other dogs suffer from different kinds of anxiety. Some, for example, are terrified of thunderstorms (a prime example: the lead canine character in the book and movie *Marley and Me*.) Others freak out when they hear construction noises. These unhappy campers cope with their problems in ways that often make their people unhappy as well. Some bark incessantly. Others can't stop panting. Still others destroy the household furniture, carpets, or walls. And some, alas, have bathroom accidents.

Unfortunately, remedial housetraining doesn't work with anxiety-ridden dogs, at least not right away. Before such a dog's housetraining problem can be solved, she needs help from experts to determine what's causing her anxiety and the resulting behavioral issues. The anxious dog's veterinarian may choose to try treating the problem himself or may refer dog and owner to either a certified applied animal behaviorist or a veterinary behaviorist. Either way, treatment of anxiety takes two tracks simultaneously: reducing the anxiety and then modifying the behavior.

To reduce the anxiety, a veterinarian may prescribe medication specifically designed to treat such problems, such as clomipramine (Clomicalm) or fluxeitine hydrochloride (Reconcile) for separation anxiety.

Another way to reduce the anxiety level is to use D.A.P., or Dog Appeasing Pheromone. This product mimics the properties of the pheromones produced by a mother dog who's nursing puppies. A diffuser plugged into an electrical outlet distributes the product throughout the room. You can obtain products that use this pheromone over-the-counter, but consulting your vet first is prudent.

After the anxiety is reduced, efforts to modify the anxious behavior can begin. For a great discussion of how this works, consult *Dog Training For Dummies,* by Jack and Wendy Volhard (Wiley). By reducing the dog's anxiety, you're likely to reduce the problematic bathroom behavior.

Picking among experts

Twenty-first century dog owners are lucky. If their pooches have problems, these owners can choose among a wide range of experts to help solve those problems. The right expert to choose depends on what the problem is and how difficult it is to solve. Here's what you need to know to find an expert to help your dog when you can't help her on your own:

- **Veterinarians:** Vets are, in essence, physicians for animals. Just as physicians for humans follow their undergraduate educations with stints in medical school and internships in hospitals, veterinarians attend veterinary school and often complete internships in veterinary clinics. A veterinarian is the first person you should consult if something appears to be amiss with your dog, either physically or behaviorally. Often, a change in your dog's behavior is a sign of a physical problem.

- **Trainers:** Trainers are individuals who specialize in teaching people how to help their dogs live happily and successfully in human households. You're most likely to find a trainer in a group obedience class, but many trainers also do private one-on-one consulting. If you're looking to teach your dog or puppy basic good manners and want to do so in a group atmosphere, look for a trainer. You can find a searchable database of dog-friendly dog trainers at the Association of Pet Dog Trainers Web site (www.apdt.com).

- **Certified applied animal behaviorists:** These folks aren't necessarily veterinarians, but they do have extensive training in a biological or behavioral science, plus professional experience in dealing with complicated animal behavior problems. These experts, who are certified by the Animal Behavior Society (ABS), can help owners deal with problems that a trainer can't solve. You can find a certified applied animal behaviorist through the searchable database at the ABS Web site (www.animalbehavior.org).

- **Veterinary behaviorists:** These are veterinarians who've completed an extensive course of training, including an internship and residency in animal behavior, after receiving their veterinary degrees and who've passed an examination given by the American College of Veterinary Behaviorists (ACVB). Unlike certified applied animal behaviorists (unless those behaviorists are veterinarians), any veterinary behaviorist can prescribe medication to deal with certain challenging behavioral problems, such as separation anxiety. Many veterinary behaviorists are affiliated with colleges of veterinary medicine or with large specialty veterinary practices. Generally, veterinarians must refer their clients to these specialists, but you can also find one by logging onto the ACVB Web site at www.veterinarybehaviorists.org and running through the site's searchable database.

However, a dog need not encounter an alligator near his bathroom to want to find a new one. Dogs can develop phobias about their potty spots or other aspects of their lives for reasons that their people can't determine. In any case, if your dog suddenly balks at using his potty place, your best bet may be to do what he wants: Find him a new place to potty. Every time he goes in that new place, reward him with lots of praise and a small treat.

At the same time, engage in some remedial housetraining. Crate the dog when you can't watch him so he doesn't continue to go in the wrong place. If you slip up and he does, clean up thoroughly and without comment. As he becomes accustomed to the new bathroom and begins going reliably in the new potty place, you can begin letting him out of the crate for longer periods.

The Dog Who Gets Distracted

Does your four-legged friend seem more interested in chasing off any squirrels or other critters who invade your backyard than in doing her business there? Does she pick up a stick for you to throw as soon as you enter the yard? If you take her for a walk, is she more likely to bark at the dog ambling on the other side of the street than to poop or pee? In other words, when it's time for your pooch to potty, does pottying appear to be the last thing she wants to do?

If so, you have the Dog Who Gets Distracted. To bring her attention back to her job — to poop or pee — you need to take on the job of minimizing distractions. If your dog gets sidetracked while out in the yard, consider walking her on the leash to her potty area until she remembers why she's supposed to be out there. If her lack of focus occurs while you're out walking her, take steps to regain her attention. For example, try turning around and walking in the opposite direction.

If your dog seems easily distracted, consider adjusting your pooch's bathroom schedule. Your dog may be uninterested in doing her duty simply because she doesn't have to go, especially if she's an older puppy who's still on a younger puppy's schedule. If your distractible friend is over 5 months of age but you're still taking her out every couple of hours, give yourself a break. Let her hold her water longer, and she'll probably do her duty more promptly when you do take her out.

The Fair-Weather Piddler

Although the U.S. Postal Service claims that neither rain nor sleet nor hail prevents the delivery of the U.S. mail, some dogs appear to believe that the onset of such weather is a perfectly natural reason to refuse to perform their outdoor duties. Alas, these pooches just don't want to do their business under less-than-ideal weather conditions.

The best way to deal with such circumstances is to leverage your dog's instincts in your favor. Any time you want him to do his business quickly, take him to the place he whizzed or pooped upon during his previous trip out. Odds are he'll smell his previous anointing and the odor will jog his memory and prompt him to perform an encore.

If taking him to his previous potty spot doesn't work, bring him to a place where you know other pooches have pottied. Most dogs confronted with other canine calling cards feel compelled to leave some of their own, no matter how inclement the weather is.

A little protection from the elements may also help, particularly with small dogs or short-haired dogs who feel the effects of rain and cold temperatures more intensely. Consider buying a raincoat and/or a sweater if your four-legged friend is one of these weather-sensitive individuals.

Finally, be prepared to brave the elements yourself if you want to be sure your dog has done her business. That means snapping on the leash and trudging through the rain or snow until your doggie downloads — or at least accompanying her to your backyard to make sure she really does what she's supposed to do.

The Bedwetter

Although most dogs will do almost anything to avoid peeing in the places where they sleep, some pooches do wet their beds. However, such behavior isn't normal, and you shouldn't treat it as such.

The bad news here is that a dog who wets her bed is invariably a dog with a medical problem; she needs to see a veterinarian as soon as possible. The good news is that the Bedwetter's problem is generally not serious and almost always is very treatable.

Among the dogs most likely to leak urine in their sleep are older spayed females. Just as older human females tend to have more trouble holding their water than their younger sisters do, such is the case with older canine females. In addition, spaying can lead to a loss of tone in the urinary tract muscles, causing the dog to dribble in her sleep. In such cases, veterinarians often prescribe a short course of either phenylpropanolamine (PPA) or diethylstilbestrol (DES), a treatment that lasts only a few days or maybe a week. The latter is a synthetic compound that has the properties of natural estrogens and can help a dowager doggie stay dry all night long.

If you're pregnant — or are trying to become pregnant — do not administer DES to your bedwetting female dog. Have someone else do it. DES has been known to cause miscarriages, birth defects, and long-term problems among human babies.

Male dogs who wet their beds at night may be suffering from urinary tract infections or kidney infections. They, too, need veterinary treatment. In most cases, the vet will ask you to bring a urine sample and will prescribe two to three weeks of antibiotics. (For tips on collecting a urine sample, see Chapter 10.)

The Dog Who Gets Amnesia

Sometimes an impeccably housetrained dog seems to suddenly forget his bathroom manners. He may pee inside the house soon after returning from a trip to his outdoor potty. He may poop or pee in front of his human companion without having asked to go out.

If your dog appears to suffer from housetraining amnesia and if he's more than 7 years of age, he may suffer from a condition called canine *cognitive dysfunction syndrome,* or CDS. The condition is very similar to human Alzheimer's disease. In addition to the loss of housetraining skills, dogs with CDS may be disoriented, appear to no longer recognize the other members of the family, and sleep more during the day but less during the night.

Any elderly dog who exhibits symptoms of CDS should be seen by a veterinarian. The vet will examine your canine companion and order lab tests that can identify other possible causes of housetraining lapses and other problems, such as kidney or liver disease. If those causes are ruled out, a CDS diagnosis is likely.

CDS isn't curable, but medication and a diet prescribed by your vet may slow its progress and alleviate some of its symptoms, including housetraining amnesia.

The Dog Who Can't Hold It

Unfortunately, some dogs can't seem to help having accidents. Sometimes simple old age is the cause: After a dog enters senior-hood (which usually starts at age 7 but can vary by breed, size, and other factors), the muscles in his urinary tract become slack, which can result in unwanted puddles. Other dogs may have suffered an injury that makes bladder control sporadic, if not impossible. Of course, you're sympathetic to such a dog's plight, but you also want to preserve your carpets and furniture and keep your house smelling fresh. What can you do?

Rule out other issues

Incontinence can result not only from old age and injury but also from conditions such as diabetes, Cushing's disease, kidney disease, urinary tract infections, and urinary stones, all of which I discuss in Chapter 10. That's why the incontinent dog's first stop needs to be at his veterinarian. The vet can perform the tests needed to rule out these and other conditions.

Find a holistic vet

Acupuncture, herbs, and homeopathy may help solve or at least improve incontinence problems in some older dogs. Some veterinarians who practice Western-style medicine may also be trained in acupuncture, but if your vet isn't one of them, check out the list at the American Holistic Veterinary Medical Association at www. holisticvetlist.com. In any case, hold off on ordering herbs or trying holistic remedies until you consult a veterinarian.

Consider diapers

If nothing else works, doggie diapers may be the way to go. Pet product manufacturers sell both washable and disposable diapers; type the term "dog diapers" into an Internet search engine, and you'll get over 80,000 hits.

Don't use any of these diaper products for dogs who are being housetrained, who suffer from submissive urination (see the earlier section "The Dog Who Pees Lying Down"), or for whom other conditions haven't been ruled out. However, if your otherwise reasonably healthy dog simply can't hold it and other solutions haven't worked, diapers can be a reasonable remedy.

The Poop Eater

Some dogs, alas, are not content to eat the food that you prepare for them. They choose to eat other items as well, ranging from the merely bizarre to the out-and-out disgusting. In the latter category is that truly gross practice that experts call *coprophagy* (but which the rest of us call poop-eating or stool-eating). That stool may come from the Poop Eater or from some other animal.

No one really knows why a Poop Eater indulges in this pastime. Although some experts have speculated that a dog who eats stool suffers from some sort of nutritional deficiency, this belief hasn't been proven. Others believe that the habit may result from anxiety or stress, particularly among dogs who spend a lot of time in kennels. Either way, the practice not only grosses out the human but can also result in a dog's ingesting parasites that may be infesting the stool.

The best way to deal with a Poop Eater is to keep him from getting to the poop in the first place. Walk your dog on a leash outdoors so you can keep him away from any poop lying on the ground. Better yet, don't leave any poop on the ground. Clean it up right away. To discourage indoor poop-eating, keep your cat's litter boxes out of your dog's reach and change all litter boxes — feline or canine — frequently.

Your vet may be able to suggest products that discourage poop eating, too — but bear in mind that you'll need to feed such products permanently to permanently end the behavior.

The Bleeding Lady, or the Canine Fertility Goddess

Is your female dog licking her private parts a lot? Do they look swollen? Is she bleeding from her vaginal area? If the answer to any of those questions is yes, your dog doesn't have a housetraining problem. Instead, she's exhibiting her canine womanhood.

That's right: Your dog is experiencing something like the canine equivalent of a human menstrual period, but there's a significant difference between the two. A human female's menstrual period generally signals that she isn't pregnant. A canine female's menstrual period — more commonly known as her heat cycle — means that she can become pregnant if she mates with a male dog within about a week.

To deal with your female dog's bloody discharge, get her some doggie diapers, which are available at most pet supply stores.

More important, though, is the need to keep your dog away from any and all male dogs if you don't want her to have puppies. After her heat cycle is over, which is about three weeks after the first bloody discharge begins, have her spayed — either with your vet or through a low-cost spay/neuter clinic. That way, you'll never again need to deal with heat cycles, overexcited male dogs, or the possibility that she could become pregnant unexpectedly. You'll also make an important contribution to eliminating the problem of pet overpopulation.

Of course, you can prevent this problem completely if you spay your female dog before her first heat cycle occurs (usually at 7 to 9 months of age). In doing so, not only will you spare yourself the mess of the heat cycle and the hassle of dealing with unwanted puppies, but you'll also significantly reduce your dog's chances of getting mammary cancer later in life.

Chapter 10

Understanding How an Oh-No Can Become a Problem-o

*A*ll too often, dogs develop potty problems that have nothing to do with whether they've mastered housetraining. Instead, these apparent bathroom boo-boos actually signal that Fido's not feeling well. Some of these bathroom-symptom illnesses are minor, but others can be serious or even life-threatening. Unfortunately, most people with pooches can't tell which is which. That's why you need to take your housetrainee to the veterinarian for a checkup if he appears to have forgotten his bathroom manners for more than a day or so.

In this chapter, I discuss some potty-related conditions and illnesses; however, remember that the list isn't inclusive. Plenty of other health problems may cause symptoms that are similar or identical to those I describe here. The bottom line: If your dog's bathroom behavior or output deviates significantly from what's normal for him, he may well be sick. Put in a call to your veterinarian.

A Whiz of a Problem

Normally, a dog takes a whiz three or four times a day after she masters proper potty protocol. Depending on what time of day she performs her anointing, her pee may be bright yellow in color (first thing in the morning) or lighter yellow (later in the day or whenever she's held it for a while). Deviations from those norms can mean your pooch isn't feeling up to par. Here are some examples of when peeing problems may signal health problems.

Constant peeing

A housetrained dog who's suddenly peeing all over the house probably hasn't developed bathroom amnesia. And if she gets to her potty spot but asks to go there every hour on the hour, her bladder hasn't suddenly shrunk. In both cases, she's probably developed a urinary tract infection, or UTI.

Although they're uncomfortable (ask any person who's gotten one!), UTIs aren't necessarily serious — if they're treated promptly. You can't doctor these infections yourself, though. Treatment begins with a visit to your veterinarian. Your vet will examine your dog, analyze a urine sample, and prescribe the antibiotics needed to knock out the infection.

Antibiotics take several days to eliminate the UTI. In the meantime, though, here's what you can do to make your canine companion more comfortable:

- **Step up the bathroom breaks.** A dog with a UTI who pees all the time is doing exactly what she needs to do: flush the infectious bacteria out of her system. So to help your UTI-ridden friend help herself, let her take as many potty breaks as she needs. If your pooch potties outside, be prepared to let her out or take her to her potty area every couple of hours or so (or if you won't be home, ask a neighbor to do so). If your dog uses papers or a litter box, make sure its location is never more than a few steps from where she is.

- **Encourage her to drink.** To encourage those potty breaks, do what you can to persuade your pooch to drink as much water as possible. Start by keeping her water dish filled with fresh water. Another good idea is to place water bowls in several areas of the house so your dog never needs to walk too far to get herself a drink.

- **Finish those meds.** Although a dog's UTI symptoms generally abate after just a couple of days on antibiotics, it's important to finish out the entire prescription, which can run as long as 21 days. That's because even though the symptoms have subsided, the infection may still be present — and stopping the meds prematurely allows it to worsen. When that happens, the symptoms return with a vengeance.

Your four-legged friend is much less likely to contract a UTI if she gets enough chances to discharge her urine. Don't ask her to hold it more than eight hours or so at a time — and if you can provide more frequent bathroom breaks, so much the better.

Constant drinking and constant peeing

A dog who suddenly starts drinking more water than usual (and consequently starts peeing more than usual) may be suffering from one of several conditions. Some of these conditions are serious, and others aren't. Here are just a few of the suspects:

- ✔ **Hot weather:** If your dog's water intake rises soon after the onset of a heat wave, you can blame the weather. During hot spells, a dog may drink more water than usual simply to maintain a normal body temperature.

- ✔ **Diabetes:** Diabetes occurs when the pancreas produces either too little insulin or poorly functioning insulin. Either way, the amount of sugar in the bloodstream rises, and the individual drinks more water to dilute the sugar. Diabetic dogs also may have ravenous appetites and often are overweight. The treatment for dogs with diabetes is the same as for humans with this disease: medication, nutritional management, and exercise.

- ✔ **Kidney problems:** When a dog's kidneys aren't functioning well, he urinates much more often than usual and can't retain the fluids his body needs. Consequently, he tries to offset the loss by drinking more water, which in turn spurs still more peeing and fluid loss. Some kidney problems are simple infections that a vet can treat with antibiotics. Others are much more serious, though, involving permanent damage to the organ. Those also require a vet's care and expertise.

- ✔ **Cushing's disease:** This condition occurs when a dog's body produces too much adrenal hormone. In addition to excessive drinking and urinating, a dog with Cushing's may also suffer from hair loss, a drooping abdomen, panting, increased appetite, and muscle weakness. Treatment depends on what's causing the overproduction of adrenal hormone in the first place.

The problem with constant drinking and peeing is that only a veterinarian can perform the tests needed to diagnose and treat a dog with such symptoms. Bottom line: Get your canine to his doctor if he's suddenly starting to pee and drink more often.

Pee that comes out slowly or not at all

Some dogs do their darndest to pee, only to have little to show for their efforts. They perform their pre-potty maneuvers, position themselves accordingly, and then release next to nothing. Maybe a drop or two emerges, if that.

 A dog who is clearly straining to pee needs to see a veterinarian right away. Your dog may well have urinary stones, which can be fatal if left untreated.

 Urinary stones form when minerals that usually pass from the dog's body when he pees clump together instead. Generally, these stones are located in the bladder, but sometimes they move to the *urethra,* which leads from the bladder to the outside of the body. If a stone is large enough, it can become trapped in the urethra, restricting or even completely blocking the urinary flow. A total blockage can cause acute kidney failure, which in turn can kill the dog.

To determine whether a dog has stones, a vet palpates the abdomen, analyzes a urine sample, and may X-ray or perform an ultrasound of the dog's abdomen. After stones are discovered, treatment depends on the type of mineral that forms the stone. Some stones respond to medicines and/or foods that change the urine's chemistry, but others need to be removed surgically.

If your vet tells you that your dog's stones are made of calcium oxalate, substitute distilled or filtered water for the tap water your dog drinks. The absence of minerals in distilled or filtered water can help prevent such stones from forming.

Oddly colored pee

A dog's pee should be yellow — although the intensity of that yellow color may vary, depending on how long ago the previous potty break was. If at any time your canine companion's urine doesn't evoke thoughts of the late Frank Zappa's notorious ditty, "Don't Eat the Yellow Snow," you need to call your vet. Here's what urine color can tell you:

- ✔ **Dark-looking urine (either rust-colored or slightly red):** This signals the presence of blood. Bloody urine may result from a urinary tract infection (see the earlier section "Constant peeing"), or it can signal an internal injury. Blood clotting disorders or urinary stones (see the preceding section) may also be the culprits. In any case, a trip to the vet is in order.

> ✔ **Very light-colored or clear urine, especially first thing in the morning:** This may mean that your dog's kidneys aren't retaining as much water for her body as they should be. Such a dog also may be peeing a lot and drinking more water than usual. Among the possible causes are diabetes, kidney disease, and Cushing's disease (see the preceding sections). Any way you look at it, though, the bottom line's the same: Get your four-legged friend to her veterinarian as soon as possible.

The Scoop on Poop Problems

A dog's poop can tell her person much about the state of that dog's health. Here are examples of when a dog's poop may be telling you that the pooper is sick.

Poop on the run (s)

Dog poop should be firm and compact, and it shouldn't stink — at least not very much. All too often, though, a dog's poop not only smells bad but also comes out fast, furious, and often. To make matters worse, it looks very runny. In other words, the dog has diarrhea.

A dog can get diarrhea for a lot of reasons. Some are serious and require a veterinarian's attention. Others aren't as big of a deal, and they respond to home care.

Young puppies with diarrhea who vomit more than once an hour over a half-day or so should see a veterinarian immediately.

If the situation isn't that urgent, here's what you can do to help reduce the runs:

1. **Forget about food for the first day.**

   If your dog has more than one runny bowel movement in a given day, hold off on feeding her for the next day or so. Your dog's digestive system, which has been working overtime, needs to take a breather. A 24-hour fast gives your canine's digestive tract the time it needs to calm down a little bit.

   Diarrhea can dehydrate a dog pretty quickly because that runny poop draws liquids from a dog's body systems. To forestall dehydration, keep fresh water available for your four-legged friend and consider placing several water bowls around your house so she can take a drink more easily.

2. **Start a bland diet after a day or so.**

    Start giving your dog some food that's easy on the tummy.
    A good foundation for a bland diet is a mixture of boiled
    rice and hamburger. Be sure to pour off any fat from the
    hamburger before you serve it to your dog; leaving in the
    grease can bring on a new round of the runs. Make sure,
    too, that food is sufficiently cool before serving so that your
    dog doesn't burn her tongue. If you don't want to cook ham-
    burger, add some lowfat cottage cheese to the rice.

3. **If your dog still has the runs after two days, call your
   veterinarian.**

    Most simple cases of doggie diarrhea abate within a day or
    two, so call your vet if the problem continues. If your dog
    is also vomiting and drinking a lot of water, call your vet
    sooner.

Soft, stinky poop

Dog poop should be formed enough so you can pick it up easily
without leaving much behind. But is your dog's poop full of mucus?
Is it really soft when you scoop it up? And does it stink to high
heaven? The cause may be a food that disagrees with your canine
companion's digestive system, or it may be the presence of a parasite. Here's how to solve either problem:

- **Look for a pattern.** If you feed your dog a varied diet, try
  to determine whether his stinky-poop episodes occur after
  he eats one particular food. For example, I noticed that my
  Golden Retriever, Allie, would produce soft, stinky, mucus-
  filled poop — not to mention become a gasbag — whenever
  I fed her canned mackerel. When I stopped feeding her the
  mackerel, her noxious gas and poop stopped, too.

- **Purge the parasite (with a vet's help).** Your dog may have
  giardia, a protozoan parasite. Besides soft stools, other symptoms of canine giardiasis include diarrhea, diminished appetite, weight loss, vomiting, and traces of blood in the stool.
  Veterinarians report that they're seeing more and more dogs
  with giardiasis, which usually spreads when a dog drinks con-
  taminated water or walks through damp areas and licks his
  feet afterward.

    As with so many other bathroom maladies, getting rid of giar-
    dia requires a veterinarian's expertise. The most common
    remedy is an antibacterial drug called metronidazole, better
    known as Flagyl.

You can help keep giardia at bay by following good sanitary practices such as washing your hands whenever you handle an infected animal. And because these unwelcome little critters thrive in damp environments, keeping the dog's living area dry is a very good idea.

Oily poop

Is your dog's poop oily and greasy-looking? Has she had diarrhea for a long time, despite the efforts of you and your veterinarian to treat her? Is her coat thin-looking? Does she look malnourished?

If so, your dog's problem may be her pancreas. This organ produces not only the hormone insulin but also special enzymes that help her body digest the nutrients in her food. Sometimes the pancreas doesn't produce enough of those enzymes, particularly those that break down the fat in foods. Consequently, the fat passes through the body and ends up in the poop, giving the stool that greasy look. A dog with this condition is suffering from *exocrine pancreatic insufficiency,* or EPI. Among the breeds that are prone to this condition are German Shepherd Dogs and Great Danes.

Many cases of EPI can be treated by putting the dog on a lowfat diet and prescribing medicines that contain the digestive enzymes the dog can't produce. But only your veterinarian can determine whether EPI is causing your dog's pooping problem, so before you do anything else, bring your dog to her doctor.

Poop that comes out slowly or not at all

If your dog's poop comes out very slowly despite his best efforts to produce some, he may be constipated — the opposite of diarrhea. Like diarrhea, constipation can signal either a minor problem or a major ailment. The trick is to know which is which. Waiting for a little while — no more than a day — should result in an answer.

Meanwhile, try the following relief-producing measures for your anal-retentive friend:

  ✔ **Give some veggies.** Many dogs enjoy getting some vegetables with their daily rations, and this is one dietary preference that can be good for your canine companion. Vegetables such as carrots, green beans, broccoli, and beets provide the bulk needed to loosen up a puppy's poop-maker. In addition, they're low in calories, which makes them terrific treats for pudgy pooches. Cook veggies and then puree them in your blender or food processor so that they're easy for your dog to eat.

Try giving your dog canned pumpkin not only to combat constipation but also to help deal with diarrhea (yes, it works for both!) and just generally keep him regular. Make sure, though, that you give your dog plain canned pumpkin, not pumpkin pie filling, which has too much sugar for dogs. Your vet can tell you how much pumpkin to serve per meal.

✔ **Lay on the liquid.** Your dog needs water to stay healthy, and extra water can soften the stool that's packed inside your pooch. Keep your friend's water dish filled with fresh, cool water — and if he's still not drinking, try placing several water bowls throughout the house.

✔ **Get him moving.** Simple constipation often clears up with some extra exercise — additional movement on the outside gets a dog's insides going, too.

✔ **Know when to get help.** If your dog's symptoms don't clear up in a day or so and he's clearly trying to take a dump, take him to your vet. He may be suffering from a bowel obstruction or other serious problem. If he begins to vomit, see your vet sooner.

Resist the temptation to feed your dog leftover cooked bones from that steak or pork chop you ate. Such bones can cause serious bowel obstructions.

Poop that contains other things

Sometimes a dog's poop consists of more than just bodily waste. In such cases, even a cursory glance can often reveal the presence of substances that are decidedly unpoopy. Those substances may result from dietary indiscretions by your dog, less-than-optimum food preparation by you, or the presence of unwanted critters in your dog's digestive system. Here are some common foreign bodies that appear in canine poop and how to deal with them.

Worms disguised as grains, sprouts, or pasta

If your dog's deposits look like they're laced with grains, sprouts, or pasta, she probably has worms. A tapeworm infestation shows up in the stool as little bits of rice. Roundworms, on the other hand, look like thin spaghetti or alfalfa sprouts. With either parasite, rely on your vet to provide proper treatment.

Even if you don't see signs of parasites in your dog's poop, have your vet check a sample of your dog's stool at least once a year for worms and other problems.

Threads or pieces of plastic

Maybe you're seeing little bits of plastic or thread in your dog's stool. If so, your buddy's probably eating his toys or some socks in addition to (or instead of) his usual fare.

Plastic toys with small parts can be especially dangerous because your dog can choke on them. Toys with squeakers can be particularly challenging if your dog swallows the squeaker. Socks may be equally hazardous because they can cause a blockage in a dog's digestive tract. Other hazards to dogs' digestive tracts include rope toys, Christmas tinsel, and all manner of poisonous plants (visit the Web site of the ASPCA Animal Poison Control Center at www.aspca. org/pet-care/poison-control for a list of toxic plants).

The best remedy here is prevention. Don't hang tinsel on your Christmas tree, bypass rope toys, keep houseplants inaccessible to your dog, and pick up socks from the floor. And make sure that your dog is playing with his toys, not eating them.

That said, if your vigilance isn't enough and your dog manages to scarf something he shouldn't, put in a call to your vet. If the dietary indiscretion consists of small pieces of a toy or a squeaker, your dog may well pass those pieces in his stool — but put in a call to your vet, just to be sure. Larger items like socks probably won't make it through and will need to be removed surgically.

Veggie chunks

If your dog likes vegetables, you may find chunks of those vegetables in your pooch's poop. That's because dogs can't absorb the nutrients in vegetables unless they're chopped up to a very fine degree. The remedy here: Sharpen your veggie-chopping skills or haul out the food processor.

Gray, black, or red poop

Although healthy canine urine is yellow in color, the color of healthy canine stool can vary considerably. Depending on what the dog has eaten and the amount of bile in her system, her poop can range from tan to dark brown in color and even sometimes be green or orange (the latter color can result when a dog eats canned pumpkin or sweet potatoes). However, some colors indicate health problems:

>   ✔ **Gray or cement in color:** Your dog may be suffering from an obstruction in her bile duct. Such obstructions can signal the presence of a gall bladder problem, a tumor, or *pancreatitis*

(inflammation of the pancreas). In any case, gray poop requires that you and your dog visit her veterinarian.

✔ **Black or very dark brown:** Your dog may be bleeding from her stomach or elsewhere in her upper digestive tract. Such stool, particularly if the poop resembles wet coffee grounds, can indicate the presence of a tumor or an ulcer. Other possible causes include kidney or liver disease, gastritis, or inflammatory bowel disease.

✔ **Red:** If you see red blood in your dog's poop, she's probably suffering from a condition of the colon or rectum, such as colitis or a tumor in the rectum.

No matter what the cause, the presence of blood in the stool indicates that a serious health problem is likely afoot. A call and visit to your vet is in order.

Skinny poop

If your dog's poop looks like thin strips, he may be suffering from a narrowing in his large intestine or his rectum. The causes may be an enlarged prostate (in intact male dogs), a mass or tumor pressing on the large intestine, or a problem from within either of those two organs. Call your veterinarian and book an appointment as soon as possible.

Gaseous Emissions

Most doggie farts result from mundane causes: eating too quickly or eating the wrong things. Here's how to turn your gasbag of a doggie into a more comfortable canine (and a better-smelling one, too!):

✔ **Slow his intake.** A dog often starts tooting if he's scarfed his meal too quickly. If your canine companion seems to inhale his meals, try feeding him from a bowl that's specifically designed to slow down his food intake. Generally, these products are divided into sections that force the dog to pause between gulps because he can't put his entire face into the bowl. Among the available products are the DogPause bowl (www.dogpausebowl.com) and the Eat Slower pet dish (www.eatslowerpetdishes.com). A similar product is the Durapet Slow-Feed Bowl, which features a raised dome in the middle of the dish.

Collecting potty samples

To figure out what may be causing a dog's potty problems, veterinarians need to analyze the pooch's bathroom output. Unfortunately, vets can't send their patients to the bathroom down the hall and ask them to pee into a cup, nor can they give them one of those stool smear sample cards to use. That means that you have to find a way to collect the poop and pee samples that your veterinarian needs to help your four-legged friend.

However, these tasks need not be daunting. To collect either urine or stool, all you need are an oblong plastic bag (such as the kinds that newspapers and bread loaves are wrapped in) and an airtight plastic container. Armed with your sampling equipment, proceed to collect your dog's urine as follows:

1. **Take your dog to her potty spot.**

2. **Pull the plastic bag over your hand and wrist.**

3. **Hold the plastic container with your bagged hand.**

4. **Watch your dog carefully, and as soon as she bends her knees (or he lifts his leg), push the container into position with your bagged hand.**

   That way, any errant dog pee splashes on the bag rather than on you.

5. **Cover the container.**

6. **Remove the bag from your hand and put it in the trash.**

7. **Bring the container to your veterinarian as soon as possible.**

Collecting a dog's poop is even easier. Here's what you need to do:

1. **Put the plastic bag over your hand.**

2. **Take your dog to her potty spot.**

3. **Watch for signs that your dog's about to do the doo, and after she's finished, pick up the poop with your bagged hand.**

4. **With the other hand, pull the bag inside out.**

   The poop is now inside the bag, at the bottom.

5. **Knot the bag with your hand.**

   If you want to, put the bagged poop in the airtight container.

The fresher the sample, the more accurate the analysis will be. Experts suggest that the sample be no more than 12 hours old — but if you keep it in the fridge or outdoors in cold temperatures, a 24-hour-old sample will be okay. If you can't get a sample or if a sterile sample is needed, your veterinarian can do the job.

Getting wind of doggie displeasure

True story: Once upon a time, many years ago, my family and I lived with a Miniature Dachshund named Casey. He was small in physical stature, but he clearly considered himself to be a big guy in every other way. As such, he appeared to believe that hopping up on the sofa and taking up the space where his humans liked to sit was perfectly okay.

One time, though, my mother disagreed and ordered Casey off the couch so she could settle in and watch some television. Casey complied but not without making his displeasure clear: As he hopped off the couch and hit the floor, he tooted. While we humans were left to deal with the stench of that toot, Casey nonchalantly trotted upstairs with nary a backward glance.

✔ **Examine his diet.** A sudden change of diet can prompt a pooch to turn on the toots. If your dog's turning flatulent, try switching him back to his old diet for a week or so. If you took him off his old diet for medical reasons, consult your vet concerning what other dietary options are appropriate for your dog.

✔ **Introduce additives.** A gassy Lassie may benefit from having activated charcoal (available at local pharmacies) or digestive-enzyme supplements added to her food. Such products can ease digestion by absorbing the gas or other materials that are irritating your dog's digestive tract and causing her to toot. Follow the instructions on the package or consult your vet to figure out how much to give.

A dog who's not only gaseous but also retching, unable to lie down, and with a larger-than-usual abdomen may be suffering from an extremely serious condition called *bloat* — the swelling and/ or twisting of the stomach. Large dogs with deep chests, such as Rottweilers, Labrador Retrievers, and Great Danes, are especially prone to this condition, but it can happen to any dog, especially if he exercises within an hour or so after a meal. This condition is fatal if not treated quickly. If your dog shows any signs of bloat, get him to the nearest veterinary clinic as soon as possible.

Chapter 11

Sorting Out Humans' Housetraining Challenges

. . . .

In This Chapter

▶ Making housetraining a family affair

▶ Managing schedules, treats, and crate time

▶ Working with dogs who are home alone or on the road

▶ Addressing household changes

▶ Housetraining a shelter or rescue dog

. . . .

Some of the challenges a puppy or dog faces during house-training are not of her making. Such challenges are generally those her humans pose. Perhaps different humans in her household have different ideas about housetraining. Perhaps the humans are putting her in her crate and expecting her to hold it for hours on end. Maybe they're giving her too many treats or not cleaning up completely when she makes a mistake.

Maybe changes in her life or the lives of her people are causing her to hit a housetraining plateau — or worse, regress. Another challenge may occur when she joins her family on a road trip, even if she's a housetraining ace. And all too often, dogs who come from rescue groups or animal shelters face special challenges as they attempt to master Housetraining 101. That's not the fault of their temporary caregivers at the shelter or in foster care, but such dogs nevertheless experience challenges over which they have little or no control.

This chapter helps you deal with special circumstances that can beset the canine housetrainee and the human members of her pack.

Suffering from potty-duty burnout

When Allie, our Golden Retriever, came to live with us as an 8-week-old puppy, my husband and daughter basically abdicated housetraining responsibilities and left them to me. I guess they figured that because I had written a manual on house-training (the 1st edition of this book), their help wasn't needed, much less wanted.

They were wrong. Oh, were they wrong. Allie needed hourly trips to the outdoor potty when she first joined our household — which, unhappily, occurred during a winter of record-breaking snowfalls. Within a week or so, I was exhausted from accompanying Allie on all those trips, and I was pretty annoyed with both Stan and Julie for foisting the whole business onto me.

One evening, while they were at the movies and I was home on housetraining duty (again!), I just snapped. I took Allie out about a half hour before they were due home. Then I put Allie in her crate and went to bed. But before I turned out the light, I wrote out a detailed schedule for the next few days listing who would be doing potty duty at which time. And I made it clear in that note that the duty roster I was creating was not negotiable.

To their credit, Stan and Julie didn't protest. They read the schedule and adhered to it, and I got some much needed rest. To this day, Stan generally takes Allie out last thing at night, and Julie's happy to take on dog-walking duties when she visits home from college.

Crafting a Family Housetraining Plan

In some ways, a person who lives alone finds housetraining much easier than people who live with other people do. If you live solo, you're the only human who's in charge of your dog's care. Unless you hire help such as dog walkers and pet sitters, you don't have to coordinate dog care tasks, including housetraining, with anyone else. The only person who can be inconsistent with housetraining is you — and you certainly won't be inconsistent, will you?

But when other people reside in your household, things get more complicated. Living with other humans gives you a choice: to be the sole caregiver (not an option I recommend) or to get the other human pack members involved in the housetraining enterprise. Here are some ways to make sure the latter option works.

Dividing duties: A plan to relieve the primary caregiver

First Lady Michelle Obama has said that she's assuming primary responsibility for taking care of the First Puppy, a Portuguese Water Dog named Bo. She has just the right attitude: She realizes that 10-year-old Malia and 7-year-old Sasha are too young to have full responsibility for taking care of their new Portuguese Water Dog, and she's committed to taking on that responsibility herself. But if Mrs. Obama is on the road with her husband or on her own, she knows she can rely on someone in the office of the White House Usher (the household staff) to step in and take Bo to his potty. Most primary doggie caregivers aren't so lucky.

Being a dog's primary caregiver shouldn't mean drawing a 24/7 housetraining detail — unless that's what the caregiver really wants to do. But if you're the primary caregiver, don't think you can do it all. You'll just end up with a boatload of resentment toward your nearest and dearest (read about my experience in the nearby sidebar). For the sake of family harmony, figure out ahead of time who will take Fifi out and when.

Getting the adults on the same page

Housetraining is next to impossible if one adult is trying to teach the pup to potty on newspaper and another wants that pup to do her business outside. Before you bring your four-legged friend home from the breeder, shelter, or rescue group, the adult members of the household need to agree on the following:

- ✔ Whether the pooch will potty outside or inside
- ✔ Which type of indoor potty your dog will use (if you all opt for the indoor option)
- ✔ Who will clean the indoor potty or pick up the poop outdoors (and when that will happen)
- ✔ Who will perform other dog care duties, such as feeding and training
- ✔ Who will clean up accidents and when

Here's the best option for who-cleans-up-when: Whoever finds the accident also cleans up that accident. Unless the accident-finder is a child under the age of 6, no one in your household should be yelling, "Mom/Honey, the dog just had an accident!" and expect Mom to come running to clean up the errant puddle or pile. And although you shouldn't expect the under-6ers to manage cleanup on their own, they should still help out when possible to discover that living with a dog involves much more than simply petting and playing with that dog.

Getting the kids on board

When President Obama and his family acquired their puppy, Bo, the president declared that everyone in the family, including daughters Malia and Sasha, would be taking turns walking the dog. He said exactly the right thing.

All the members of the family who can care for the family pet need to do so, starting with housetraining. That's why you need to make sure that every member of the family agrees to the family dog-care plan before that dog joins the family.

That said, I don't think having children under the age of 6 assume the dog-walking share of family housetraining responsibilities is a good idea. A growing pup can be way too strong for an under-6er to handle — and even if the puppy is small, most kids in that age range simply aren't ready for that sort of responsibility. Have kids that age help with other tasks, such as feeding, training, and accident cleanup — but always under adult supervision. My daughter helped her dad and me with cleanup duty when she was going into first grade and we were housetraining our Sheltie, Cory, and she came with me to Cory's puppy kindergarten classes.

Your kids may beg and plead for the new dog to sleep in the same rooms that they do. Resist such begging and pleading — at least for now — and have the dog sleep in your room. That way, you'll be more likely to hear if the dog gets restless, whines, or otherwise indicates that she needs a middle-of-the-night potty break. After your canine companion becomes a housetraining ace, perhaps you can reconsider the dog's sleeping assignment.

Most experts say — and I totally agree — that you should never leave children age 6 or younger alone with a dog. If an adult can't be there to supervise interactions between a child and a dog, confine the dog to a safe place, such as a crate.

Balancing Crate Time

After your dog becomes a housetraining ace, you can generally let her go in and out of the crate as she pleases. But during the housetraining process, you often need to close the door. You can misuse the crate in two ways when housetraining: using the crate too much and not using it enough.

Responding to accidents in her crate

If your dog has an accident in her crate, first blame yourself. No dog potties in her den if she can possibly avoid doing so. Next, try to figure out what happened:

✔ **Did you leave her in her crate for too long?** Promise yourself — and your dog — that you won't do that again.

✔ **Is she sick?** A crate with loose stool can indicate that your pooch isn't feeling well. Check out Chapter 10 for the scoop on dealing with loose poop.

✔ **Is the crate too big?** A crate should allow your dog to stand up, turn around, and lie down comfortably, but it shouldn't be much bigger than that. If your puppy's in a crate that allows her to sleep at one end and eliminate at the other, you're defeating the purpose of the crate.

✔ **Has she done it before?** If so, maybe you didn't clean up the crate completely from the previous potty transgression. Take the crate outside and hose it down. Scrub the inside with a cleaner meant especially for removing pet stains and odor. Replace any bedding, including the cushions and blankets.

Finally, don't beat yourself up. A dirty crate, although unpleasant and undesirable for both pooch and person, does occur on occasion (Yes, I'm speaking from personal experience. No, I won't share the details.) Follow the steps here, and your dog's latest crate accident should be her last.

With your dog safely in her crate-den, you can take your eyes off her, allowing you to leave the house, take a shower, pay the bills, or otherwise keep your household running. The crate time also helps the housetraining process along. By keeping your house-trainee in her crate when you can't watch her, you tap into her desire to refrain from dirtying her domicile — and as she gets refraining practice, she develops the physical control she needs to become a housetraining graduate.

However, being in the crate can be cruel to a dog if you leave her in there for too long. If you're away all day, you can't leave your housetrainee in her crate the whole time and expect her to hold it. You need to find ways to give her some relief (I discuss some options in the next section).

So what's the right balance of crate time? Chapters 6 and 7 provide some example housetraining schedules that account for time in the crate, potty breaks, and time to play or just hang out with the family.

Relieving the Home-Alone Dog

If you're training your pooch to potty indoors and her potty is accessible to her at all times, you don't need to make arrangements to relieve your home-alone dog. But if your dog is an outdoor housetrainee, you can't expect her to hold her water or the other stuff while you're away all day. Until you know that your four-legged friend is a housetraining ace (Chapter 8 helps you figure that out), you need to provide her with some daytime relief, literally. This section suggests some ways to do that.

If none of the options for relieving your home-alone dog are available five days a week, maybe you can combine them: work from home one or two days a week, go home for lunch one day or two days a week, ask a neighbor for help one or two days a week, or try some other combination.

Getting a pet-sitter or dog walker

If your dog hasn't mastered basic bathroom manners yet, one way to help her do so is to hire a pet-sitter or dog walker who can come to your home one or more times per day and take your pooch out to potty. Dog owners who reside in major metropolitan areas or their surrounding suburbs can find plenty of qualified pet-sitters, dog walkers, or pet-sitting companies by logging on to an online classified Web site such as Craigslist (www.craigslist.org). Your local newspaper's classifieds or telephone book may also offer listings. Still another pet-sitting option may be to enlist the assistance of a dog-loving neighbor who's home during the day.

Can't find help through the classifieds? Don't have a dog-loving at-home neighbor? Visit the Web site of Pet Sitters International (www.petsit.com/locate) or the National Association of Professional Pet Sitters (www.petsitters.org), type in your zip code, and find an accredited pet-sitter or pet-sitting company in your area. Both of those sites also contain valuable information on how to choose a pet-sitter.

Bringing your dog to work

Many companies allow employees to bring their dogs to work with them; maybe yours is one. Check with the Human Resources department at your company and see whether your workplace has a pet policy that allows you to bring your puppy or dog-in-housetraining (some companies specify that housetraining must be completed before your canine companion can join you in the office). If you get the green light, bring your dog, some toys, a water dish, a leash, and a crate with you. You'll find that following your dog's schedule in the office is just about as easy as it is at home.

If you're looking for a new job and want to find a dog-friendly work-place, visit Simply Hired at www.simplyhired.com. Depending on the type of job you're looking for, you can turn on a "Dog-Friendly Companies" filter and find a place to work that lets you bring your four-legged friend with you.

Going home for lunch

If your workplace is close to your home and you have an hour or so for lunch, consider going home at lunchtime and taking your pooch out for a potty break. Eat lunch at your desk either before or after the trip.

Working from home

Maybe your job allows you to telecommute, at least temporarily. If you spend most of your workday in front of a computer and/ or on the phone, see whether your company allows you to work from home, at least during your canine companion's house-training stage. Of course, if you're self-employed and chained to a computer or phone (like I am), your only task is to add your dog's housetraining schedule to your daily to-do list.

Creating a potty-proof home-alone area

If none of the preceding options are available at all, reconcile yourself to not having your puppy trained to potty exclusively outdoors — at least not right away. If you or someone else can't spell her during the day, you need to give your puppy an indoor potty to use even though you're training her to do her business outside. Here's how this method works:

- ✔ **For when you're going to be away for several hours:** Create an indoor home-alone area for your puppy — preferably someplace that doesn't have a carpet and is easy to clean. The kitchen, laundry room, or bathroom works well here. Cover the entire floor area with several layers of newspaper. Put the puppy's crate and dishes at one end; leave the door to the crate open. Use baby gates or an exercise pen to enclose the entire area so your pup can't venture beyond the room.

✔ **For when you're home:** If your puppy has pooped or peed on the papers, clean them up without comment when you arrive home. She hasn't done anything wrong by eliminating on the papers, but you don't want her to think that you want her to use the papers over the long term. Don't lay down new papers. Anytime you're home, remove the papers and follow the outdoor training instructions in Chapter 6.

✔ **For short trips out:** If you need to head out on a quick errand or otherwise can't watch your little darling, you don't need to set up the home-alone area again — put her in her crate.

Eventually, when your puppy nears 6 months of age or so, you'll be able to bypass the papers forevermore. You'll know she's ready to become a totally outdoor-trained dog when you repeatedly come home from work at night and find nothing on the papers.

Sticking to the Schedule

Most of the time, you're probably very good about getting home at midday to give your puppy-in-housetraining a much-needed potty break, but perhaps you just plain forgot today. Or maybe you decided to meet friends after work at the local watering hole without stopping to think that your pooch needed to, well, let go of some water.

In such instances, you shouldn't be surprised to find a little puddle or pile waiting for you when you get home, nor should you be angry at the individual who deposited that puddle or pile. You, not your puppy or dog, are the one who screwed up, because you didn't stick to the potty schedule you established.

That schedule conditions your canine companion to eat, drink, poop, and pee at certain times, and it helps you anticipate when he needs to eliminate, thus preventing accidents. The schedule also helps him learn to hold his pee and poop until you get home to give him the potty break he's come to expect. But if you don't show, he'll still need to go. He'll pass his personal can't-hold-it-anymore threshold and have no choice but to perform a doggie download.

And even when your dog is fully housetrained, you still need to take his needs into consideration when you make plans that don't include him. The next time you want to take advantage of a local establishment's Happy Hour on the way home from work, ask yourself whether you could refrain from doing your bathroom business for as long as you're asking your dog to refrain from doing so. If the answer is no, then do yourself and your dog a favor: Go home and give him a chance to do his business.

Bottom line here: Whenever possible, stick with the schedule that you've created for your housetraining student. You and the student will both be glad you did.

Managing Snacks

I'm a firm believer in positive reinforcement training. The old ways of teaching dogs — choke collars, harsh leash corrections, or the *alpha rolls* that required humans to roll dogs onto their backs in order to impose some sort of discipline — are dangerous to humans, not to mention incredibly stressful to the dog. I'd much rather catch a dog doing something right and reward her when she does. Most dogs think the best reward is a tasty treat.

As I note in Chapters 6 and 7, rewarding your beginning house-trainee with a treat whenever she potties in the proper place is a great way to persuade her to continue pottying in that place. But that treat needs to be very small for two reasons: first, so she doesn't put on too much weight and second, so that the treats don't wreak havoc with her bathroom schedule. In other words, too many treats are likely to put on too many pounds and prompt too many trips to the potty — or even accidents if she can't get to the potty in time. What size of treat is small enough? As tiny as you can make it.

 If, despite your efforts, your pooch is porking out by ingesting too many treats, reduce the sizes of the portions you serve her at mealtimes. Alternatively, check out the info on low-calorie treats in Chapter 4.

Messing Up the Cleanup

True story: Years before I began writing about dogs and their care, I had the pleasure of interviewing one of our nation's best-known etiquette experts and observers of social goings-on. I arrived at her home and rang the doorbell, and the expert herself opened the door, graciously inviting me inside. As I stepped into her well-appointed foyer, one of her teeny-tiny dogs ran up to me and piddled on the floor in front of me. I offered to help clean up the resulting puddle, and she accepted the offer. While I broke open some paper towels, she went to get something to clean the floor with. Unfortunately, that something was club soda. And during our interview, the expert acknowledged with some embarrassment that her dog often peed on that spot. She couldn't understand why.

But at least the expert knew that the puddle needed to be cleaned up right away. So often, dog owners forget to do that. Maybe you really meant to clean up the little puddle that your canine companion left on your carpet. But before you could get the pet stain cleaner, a telemarketer called, or your teenage daughter came home from school bemoaning how awful her school day was, or worst of all, *your* household toilet overflowed (that would be ironic, wouldn't it?). Now, a few hours later, you see your four-legged friend performing an encore on the very same spot where he left the earlier puddle.

Why did the expert's dog pee on the same spot time after time? And why would any dog want to pee in the same place she'd peed on earlier?

In the first instance, the expert wasn't using the right cleaner. Club soda may appear to remove a pet stain, but it doesn't remove the odor. The lingering scent was like a magnet to her dog, practically screaming, "Come pee again! Right here!" In the second instance, your failure to clean up at all had the same effect as the expert's failure to use the right cleaner.

The lessons here are simple: Clean up your dog's bathroom boo-boos as soon as possible after those boo-boos have occurred, and when you do, use a commercial cleaner designed specifically to remove pet stains and odor. Otherwise, you're sabotaging your efforts to housetrain your dog and you're setting her up to fail.

Anticipating Lapses Due to Household Changes

Dogs are social animals, and they don't always respond well to changes in their pack. A change in your household — such as a romantic breakup, the death of a family member (human, canine, or feline), or the departure of a child for college — can wreak havoc with your dog's bathroom manners.

If you anticipate a change in your household or are undergoing one, act now to keep your pooch from pottying in the wrong place. Here are some ideas:

✔ **Limit access.** If your dog is doing his business in the same indoor place every day, limit his access to that place. Close the door, block the spot with some chairs — do what you must to keep him from reaching that spot.

The bathroom blues

Years ago, in my single days, my dog Molly and I lived for a year with another person and his dog. When that arrangement ended, my roommate and the roommate's dog moved out, and Molly promptly developed what appeared to be housetraining amnesia.

Every day when I came back from work, I found a little puddle next to a spot where the other dog had liked to spend much of his time. I cleaned up the spot as best I could — but because I knew much less about housetraining than I do now, I thought club soda would do the trick. It didn't, and Molly kept going back to the same spot and leaving a puddle.

Finally, a light bulb went off in my head. I closed the door to the room that Molly was using for an indoor potty. That ended Molly's bathroom boo-boos — but not soon enough for me to avoid losing the security deposit to the place where I was living when Molly and I moved out.

- ✔ **Keep up routines.** As much as possible, maintain your dog's regular routine. Feed, walk, and play with him at the same times every day.

- ✔ **Up the exercise.** Trainers often say that a tired dog is a good dog, and they're right. If your four-legged friend gets sufficient aerobic exercise, he's more likely to sleep than leave his mark in the wrong spot.

- ✔ **Call the vet.** If your dog continues to potty in forbidden areas despite your taking the preceding steps, he may be sick. Have your vet check him out for a urinary tract infection or other health problem.

Helping the Newly Adopted Housetrainee

If you've adopted an adolescent or adult dog from an animal shelter or rescue group, props to you! You've saved at least two lives: that of the homeless dog whom you've welcomed into your household and that of another homeless dog who will take her place at the shelter or rescue group — hopefully just before she finds her forever home, too.

Shelters and rescue organizations point out that many of the dogs they put up for adoption are already housetrained — and in many cases, that's true. But in my experience, assuming that the dog you adopt is one of them is not a good idea. Even a dog who's been a housetraining ace may regress as she negotiates the changes from being abandoned or surrendered to the shelter or rescue group, adjusts to the shelter or foster home, and then adjusts yet again when you adopt her.

I strongly suggest that you assume that, at the very least, your newly adopted dog is going to need some housetraining help, if not start from square one on the path to understanding proper potty protocol. Here's how to give your shelter or rescue dog that help:

✔ **Get her a den.** Ideally, this den is a crate, but if your new family member doesn't take to a crate — or if you're going to have to be away all day — create a living area such as what I describe in Chapter 3.

✔ **Decide where her bathroom will be.** If your adoptee is very small, consider training her to potty in a designated indoor bathroom area. Otherwise, plan on taking her outside to do her business. Either way, check out Chapter 3 for indoor and outdoor potty placement pointers.

✔ **Create a schedule.** The adolescent or adult dog doesn't need to potty nearly as often as a young puppy does, but she still needs a consistent schedule so that she can figure out how to regulate her potty urges. Until you're able to see just how well housetrained she is, plan on taking her out first thing in the morning, last thing at night, immediately after being confined to her crate or living area, after naps, after playtime or a chewing session, and after each meal. Chapter 6 offers a sample housetraining schedule for an adult dog.

✔ **Supervise, supervise.** Until you know how well your adoptee can regulate her bathroom behavior, she needs your close supervision at all times, except when she's in her crate or living area. Keep a close eye on her when she's not being confined. That way, you figure out what she's likely to do before she deposits a puddle or pile, which can help you anticipate when she's about to do the doo.

A good way to keep an eye on your dog as you go from room to room is to attach a leash and take her with you wherever you go in the house.

✔ **Take care with her diet.** Find out what your dog ate during her stay at the foster home or shelter and get a week's supply of the same food. You can keep feeding her the same food or gradually switch her over to a regimen that you prefer. If you opt to make a switch, do it gradually over several days. An abrupt switch can upset your adoptee's stomach, which may result in diarrhea or other disruptions in housetraining.

✔ **Expect accidents.** With the excitement and stress of adjusting to a new home, your new friend is bound to make a couple of bathroom mistakes. (This is especially likely if your dog has just been spayed or neutered.) If you're lucky, you can catch her in the act, distract her, and hurry her to her potty spot. If you find an accident after the fact, just clean up calmly and completely and resolve to keep a closer eye on her next time.

✔ **Reward bathroom successes.** Take your adoptee to the same potty spot for each and every pit stop until she gets the hang of housetraining — and every time she potties at the right spot, give her a very small treat and lots of loving praise.

✔ **Be patient.** Some dogs take longer to figure out proper potty protocol than others. If your dog is over 6 months of age, a good rule of thumb is to consider your dog fully housetrained if she hasn't had an accident for a month or so.

✔ **Watch for problems.** If your adoptee is doing well with house-training but suddenly regresses for more than a day or so — or if her output is clearly not normal for the same amount of time — she may be sick. The same may be true if her bath-room behavior suddenly changes. Either way, put in a call to your veterinarian and check out Chapter 10, which outlines a number of maladies that masquerade as housetraining lapses.

Hitting the Road with Your Housetraining Graduate

Some of the best times I've had with my dogs have been when I've traveled with them. I have especially fond memories of traveling with Allie from my home in Virginia to a very special place in Vermont called Camp Gone to the Dogs, where she and I bunked together at night and engaged in all kinds of activities during the day: hiking, swimming, *lure coursing* (a sport in which a dog chases a scented lure that's attached to a string), *freestyle* (a relay race that requires the dog to retrieve a ball and jump over hoops), and even, at one unforgettable juncture, sheep herding (Allie was very interested in the sheep but hadn't a clue as to what to do with them).

However, all the excitement of going to camp — plus the extra treats and change of food involved with traveling to a training camp — wreaked havoc on Allie's digestion. About midway through each visit to camp, she and many of the other canine guests developed loose stools and some memorable flatulence. Although Allie never made a bathroom boo-boo during our stays at camp, we did make a lot of extra trips outdoors so she could potty, and scooping up all her poop was definitely more of a challenge than normally is the case.

Allie and I don't do camp anymore, but we continue to travel together — mainly to visit my mother, who lives about 200 miles away from us. Here's what I do to keep Allie's bathroom behavior on an even keel when we hit the road:

- **Limit dietary changes.** When Allie and I went to camp, I had to change her diet from raw food to canned because I couldn't keep the raw food fresh at camp. Going to visit my mom, though, is a different story; I bring the same raw food that Allie eats at home. I pack it frozen and it defrosts on the trip, ready to serve when we arrive.

- **Step up bathroom breaks.** The excitement of travel seems to make Allie want to go more often, and I accommodate that desire as best I can. She gets a potty break just before we leave, about two hours into the trip, and when we arrive at my mom's.

If you're staying at a pet-friendly hotel with your dog, give her extra pit stops until you see whether the new, temporary digs are affecting her behavior, bathroom or otherwise.

- **Pack extra poop bags.** Chances are the places where you take your dog to potty won't have poop bags at the ready, so bring your own.

- **Bring the comforts of home.** In an unfamiliar place, your dog may appreciate the familiarity of her crate, particularly when you're not with her. The crate also helps her control her bathroom urges. If your dog is trained to potty indoors, bring the indoor potty with you as well.

- **Pack some pumpkin.** No one knows exactly why, but canned pumpkin (just plain — not sugar-heavy pumpkin pie filling) does wonders to regulate your dog's pooping. Amazingly, the stuff balances out both diarrhea and constipation. For Allie, who weighs 70 pounds, I add about 4 ounces to each meal.

- **Bring along a pet stain cleaner.** My late Sheltie, Cory — who otherwise was practically a housetraining genius — developed a bad habit of marking new territory, which proved embarrassing whenever we traveled to someone's house. I carried a small bottle of pet stain cleaner with me when we ventured elsewhere, which helped restore my hosts' good opinion of him and of me.

Part IV
The Part of Tens

The 5th Wave   By Rich Tennant

In this part...

Sometimes housetraining poses more of a challenge than you anticipated. All too often, though, those challenges result from mistakes you make in teaching toileting tactics. In this part, you get ten ideas on how to avoid housetraining errors — and in case the going gets really rough, a list of ten incentives to continue the housetraining process until your dog's bathroom mistakes are a thing of the past. I wrap up with an appendix listing some top-notch Web sites, books, and magazines that offer more information on canine health, training, and companionship.

Chapter 12

Ten Housetraining Mistakes You Don't Have to Make

*H*ousetraining a puppy or dog can be a real challenge. A well-meaning but unprepared person can find plenty of opportunities to mess up the job. Some of these mistakes result from owner misunderstanding, and others occur due to owner impatience. However, any of these mistakes can make your canine companion's housetraining learning curve a lot steeper than it needs to be.

In fact, just about all housetraining mistakes are avoidable — if you know ahead of time what the possible pitfalls are. This chapter describes ten common housetraining boo-boos, why they occur, and how you can avoid making them.

Thinking the Crate Is Cruel

If your love for dogs began when you started watching TV shows such as *Lassie* when you were a kid, the idea of putting your dog in a crate probably takes a little getting used to. The image of Timmy and his glorious Collie wandering over rolling hills of farmland just doesn't square with the idea of confining your Fido in a plastic or wire enclosure until he masters his potty manners. In fact, you may feel that in doing so, you're putting Fido in a cage. "Dogs don't belong in cages," you may protest. "It's cruel." But if Fido could speak for himself, he'd probably disagree with you.

Many dogs actually love their crates. To most canine companions, the crate is the safe, secure den they instinctively long for. The crate-den offers protection from hazards such as out-of-control children and big, noisy vacuum cleaners. It also makes a terrific home away from home for the traveling canine. For most dogs, then, the crate is not an object of cruelty but an object to be appreciated.

And for people who love those dogs, the crate can be a dandy housetraining tool. Using a crate for housetraining just prompts a dog to do what comes naturally. When you confine your canine-in-housetraining to a crate during those times that you can't watch her, you tap into her inborn desire to refrain from eliminating in the den. She'll hold her pee or poop until she can leave, helping her develop bowel and bladder control. Meanwhile, she's happy and secure while lounging in her beloved den. It's a classic win-win situation — about as far from cruelty as one can get.

Some dogs do take a while to appreciate their crates. A very gradual introduction can help such a pooch discover the joys of chilling out in this makeshift den. See Chapter 5 for tips on turning your crate-phobic pooch into a crate-loving canine.

Being in the crate can be cruel to a dog in one instance: When he's left in there for too long. Don't leave your dog in his crate all day while you're at work. If you're concerned about destructiveness, enclose him in a dog-proofed room, hire someone to come walk him during the day, or take him to doggie day care. (See Chapter 11 for details on these solutions and some other options.)

Getting a Crate That's Too Big

Getting an oversized crate is a common mistake among people who've acquired young puppies and are hoping to economize on crate purchases. Such individuals buy a crate that's sized for an adult dog, not a canine youngster. The idea is that the puppy will have plenty of room to grow into his crate and the owner will have to shell out for a crate only once. Unfortunately, not only does the puppy have plenty of room to grow, but he also has enough room to sleep at one end of the crate and eliminate at the other. That defeats the purpose of the crate, which is to help the puppy develop bowel and bladder control.

A crate that's too big is a little bit like a pair of shoes that are too big. The wearer finds the shoes very comfortable, as long as he's not moving. But after he does start walking, it's clear the shoes fail to fulfill their intended purpose: to provide protection and support to the feet. Similarly, a too-big crate is certainly comfortable for a puppy, but it doesn't represent the cozy den he needs to learn to control his pooping and peeing. The solution to this problem is to buy the correct size of crate.

A crate is sized correctly when it's just big enough for a dog to stand up, turn around, and lie down.

So does a new puppy owner have to run up his credit card balance by purchasing a new crate every time his puppy shows significant growth? Not at all! You can still get away with buying just one crate that fits little Fido's expected adult size. Just buy a wire crate that comes with a divider. As your puppy grows, you can move the divider farther and farther toward the back of the crate. That way, the crate fulfills its purpose, but you have to buy one only once.

Failing to Stick to the Schedule

For the puppy or dog who's still being housetrained, sticking to the schedule is crucial to success. That's because as soon as you establish a schedule, your puppy expects to eat, drink, and eliminate at certain times. That expectation helps you anticipate when she needs to go and thus reduces the number of accidents she has. It also helps her develop enough bowel and bladder control to keep her from eliminating until it's time for the potty break she's come to expect. If she doesn't get that break, though, she may not be able to hold her water. She may pass her personal point of endurance and have no choice but to unload.

That may also be true of the housetraining graduate. No dog can keep her floodgates shut forever. If you expect your dog to refrain from eliminating during the day, you can't reasonably expect her to continue to refrain during the evening. The next time you're tempted to stop off someplace else before going home to take your dog out, ask yourself this: Could you hold it as long as she's been holding it today? If the answer is no, hightail it home and give your friend her break.

Failing to Clean Up Completely

Canine urine is a magnet to dogs — including the dog from whom the urine came. Even one stray drop can lure a dog to a given area and prompt him to pee there again.

Using club soda and/or ammonia may get rid of urine stains, but it certainly doesn't get rid of the odor. That come-hither fragrance works its dubious magic on dogs, drawing them back to the scenes of their potty crimes. If you use ammonia, not only do you fail to get rid of the odor — you actually intensify it! That's because ammonia smells a lot like urine to most dogs.

If your pooch makes a potty mistake, clean it up completely — and use a commercial cleaner that's expressly designed for the job. Otherwise, you may as well tell your dog that flunking Housetraining 101 is okay.

Not Cleaning the Indoor Potty

No question — life sometimes feels like a never-ending to-do list. Understandably, you'd like nothing better than to pare that list down a little bit. But failing to change your indoor trainee's soiled indoor potty — whether that potty is newspapers, a litter box, a grate-covered tray, or another device — should not be one of the tasks you skip.

Do you like using a dirty bathroom? Of course not. Chances are, even if the rest of your house looks like a hurricane swept through it, your bathroom is reasonably clean. And even though you probably don't enjoy cleaning your toilet, you do it anyway — because the very thought of using a dirty john grosses you out.

Your dog doesn't like to use a dirty bathroom, either. The idea of pooping or peeing on soaked papers, in a dirty litter box, or on a waste-filled bathroom tray grosses *him* out. But because he can't change his papers or litter or clean the tray himself, he's left with only one alternative to using the canine equivalent of a dirty toilet: doing his business someplace else. That solves the dirty-toilet problem for him, but it represents a housetraining setback for both of you.

Change your indoor trainee's papers or litter as soon as possible after your pooch has used them. That way, he'll stay on track with housetraining. And for advice on washing the indoor potty, flip to Chapter 7.

Thinking Your Dog Looks Guilty

You're on your way home after a long day grappling with office politics and are looking forward to spending time with your cherished canine companion. But when you walk in the door, you see a telltale stain on your gorgeous Oriental rug. When you cast a baleful glance over to your now not-so-cherished companion, he seems to wilt in front of you: He folds his ears back, places his tail between his legs, and looks away from you.

"Aha!" you think. "He knows he's been bad. He knows that he shouldn't have peed on my rug. He feels so guilty he can't even look at me."

Time out. Your dog's failure to meet your gaze does not result from guilt. His low-hanging ears and tail do not reflect remorse. His body language does not reflect any feelings he has from peeing on your rug. Before you walked in the door, he was probably taking a nap and wasn't thinking at all about how the rug got that stinky yellow stain. Only when you sent that menacing glance his way did he realize that he might be in trouble.

Dogs don't know the meaning of guilt. Your dog has no idea that you're angry because he used your Oriental rug as a potty. He doesn't even remember having done so. He understands only that you're unhappy, and he's responding in the only way that he knows how: with submissive behavior.

Scolding Her after the Fact

Scolding your dog for a housetraining error does nothing to teach her what you want her to do. If you yell at her, restrict her, or try to correct her for producing that puddle, she won't have the faintest idea why you're acting that way. She'll learn nothing from your rant except to be afraid of you.

So when you confront a misplaced puddle or pile, take a deep breath and then just zip it while you clean up. Understand that the mistake was yours, not your dog's — and figure out how to prevent that mistake from recurring.

However, if you catch your dog in the act of making a mistake, or just about to make one, your approach should be different. Distract her by clapping your hands, saying "Oops!" in a loud voice, or using a similar technique. She'll probably stop what she's doing (or what she's about to do). When she does, get her to her potty spot pronto. Then, when she unloads, praise her lavishly and give her a small treat if you have one handy.

Rubbing His Nose in You-Know-What

Back in the days of yore, people thought they could correct a dog for housetraining lapses no matter how long ago those lapses occurred. Many of those same people also thought that rubbing the offending pooch's nose in his poop or pee would further help him understand that doing his biz in the house was not a good thing to do.

But that really isn't the case. Giving the dog a snoutful of dog doo falls in the same category as thinking a dog looks guilty. Either way, dogs don't remember their housetraining mistakes. They don't feel bad for doing what comes naturally. And they don't connect having to eyeball their waste with having deposited that waste in the wrong place a few minutes or hours earlier.

If you come upon a puddle or pile inside your house, it's too late to do anything but clean it up. Do that, resolve to prevent future accidents, and consign the nose-rubbing routine to where it belongs: the past.

Changing the Menu Abruptly

You've been feeding Rover pretty much the same things day in, day out for the past few weeks, and his housetraining's been coming along beautifully. In fact, you can't quite remember the last time you had to clean up a canine potty mistake.

Then, lo and behold, it's time to celebrate Thanksgiving or another holiday that calls for a grand and glorious feast for the human members of the family. But as you're preparing that feast, the nonhuman member of the family lays an incredibly effective guilt trip on you. As you baste that turkey or prepare that sausage stuffing, Rover's there with you, staring at you and the food with big, hungry eyes. And you ask yourself how you can possibly stuff yourself with such wonderful food but force Rover to stick with his usual fare. You think, "What the heck?" and decide to give Rover a Thanksgiving dinner, too. And he loves it. He practically inhales it.

Unfortunately, several hours later, Rover has a loose, runny bowel movement all over your floor. Your tender-hearted gesture at dinnertime has given Rover an exceptionally tender tummy now — with all-too-predictable results.

Any time you change a dog's menu suddenly, you risk upsetting his digestive system. Digestive upsets in dogs manifest themselves the same way as they do for people: with diarrhea.

Does this mean that Rover can't enjoy Thanksgiving dinner along with the rest of the family? No. It does mean, though, that giving Rover a completely different meal all at once is likely to wreak havoc with his bathroom behavior. Let him have a little taste of the turkey (white meat, no skin). That way, he'll get to enjoy some holiday fare without having to pay for it afterward.

The same principle applies when you're switching Rover's every-day cuisine. If you're changing dog foods or switching from com-mercial to raw or home-prepared meals, don't make the change all at once. Do so over a period of several days so that Rover's digestive system can become accustomed to the new grub. By taking your time with any culinary changes, you'll greatly reduce the risk of messy digestive upsets.

Declaring Victory Prematurely

Oh, you are *so* proud of your little Fifi, aren't you? She's been with you for only a month, she's just 3 months old, and she hasn't had an accident for a whole week. Surely she's a housetraining prodigy. How many other dogs her age have aced their bathroom lessons so quickly and so thoroughly? Probably not many — including Fifi.

When it comes to housetraining, declaring victory prematurely is a big mistake. Being sure that those potty lessons are imprinted onto the canine brain takes longer than a week, particularly with a puppy. For one thing, a 3-month-old puppy doesn't have enough physical bowel and bladder control to be considered reliable for long periods of time. Even adult housetrainees who *have* developed that control may have trouble remembering where and when they're supposed to potty.

With canine children as well as with human children, don't give too much freedom too soon. The parents of a 5-year-old child who's figured out how to ride a bike aren't likely to let that child ride alone to the other side of town. Similarly, your canine child's housetraining prowess does not merit unsupervised access to the whole house. Give her longer stretches of unsupervised time outside her crate, or try taking her out for potty breaks a little less often. With both kids and puppies, gradually increased privileges get better results than total immediate freedom.

Chapter 13

Ten Reasons Housetrained Dogs Live in Happier Households

. . . .

In This Chapter
▶ Understanding why housetrained dogs are happier dogs
▶ Seeing why owners enjoy housetrained dogs more

. . . .

Sometimes — generally when you're cleaning up the umpteenth accident your puppy's made on your favorite area rug — you may wonder whether she's *ever* going to master the art of proper potty deportment and whether you should continue trying to teach her that art. That's when you need this chapter. Flip through these next few pages for the incentive you need to persevere.

The Houses Smell Nicer

Porta-Potties are a necessary invention, but don't you just hate using them? I do — because they stink. The initial assault on your sense of smell when you open the door is, well, intense. Keeping that example in mind, think of how stinky your entire home will be if your canine companion doesn't figure out that your home is not his personal potty. If that unpleasant thought doesn't renew your determination to housetrain your hound, think of how much money you'll save on air fresheners after that hound becomes a housetraining ace.

The Owners Save Money

Being able to cut back on, if not eliminate, purchases of canine cleanup products isn't the only way owners of housetrained dogs save money. They also use far fewer paper towels, and they can let a lot more time elapse between either professional carpet cleanings or the cleanings they do themselves. The result: extra bucks they can blow on something fun, put into savings, or use to pay off their credit card bills. What's not to like?

The Owners Are Less Cranky

I admit it: Writing about housetraining is fun. What other way could a middle-aged author be paid to get back in touch with her inner 8-year-old and contemplate bathroom matters? That said, not even I find actually dealing with the complications and messes of housetraining very much fun. Even now that I'm a so-called expert on the subject, actually housetraining a dog isn't on my list of favorite things to do. If my Golden Retriever, Allie, could talk, she'd tell you how cranky I was until she figured out where and when she was supposed to do her business.

And wouldn't you be happier if you didn't have to deal with soaking up puddles and picking up piles of doggie download? Of course you would. So invest in your future happiness, and keep plugging away at your dog's bathroom lessons. If you do, he'll eventually see the light. I promise.

The Dogs Aren't Scared When Their Owners Come Home

Coming home to a stinky puddle of pee or pile of poop isn't fun. Such olfactory greetings are bound to displease the person walking through the door. And because you're all too human, you may all too often let your dog know that you're upset — even though you've resolved only to praise your dog when he does something right, not berate him when he's done something wrong.

Dogs are very observant. After just a few of your cranky home-comings, they figure out that the sound of the key in the lock will be followed shortly thereafter by their people speaking loudly, looming over them, and being more than a little intimidating. So when that key turns, the observant dog tries to forestall his person's crankiness. He launches into Doggie Appeasement Mode: tail between the legs, ears back, cowering on the floor, rolling onto his back. He may even perform the ultimate canine appeasement gesture: peeing on the floor — not exactly what you wanted, is it?

There's just one catch: These observant dogs have no idea why their owners are cranky. They don't make the connection between their bathroom transgressions and their owners' reactions. They're just thinking, "Oh Mommy/Daddy, please don't be angry. I'll do anything, anything."

So while your housetrainee is still figuring out when and where to do the doo, try not to scare him with an outburst of annoyance or anger when you come in the door and find an unwelcome little something. Better still, get your dog housetrained so that you'll no longer be cranky when you come home and your dog will no longer be scared when your key turns in the lock.

The Owners Don't Worry about Stepping in You-Know-What

Ever hear of Wet Sock Syndrome? That's when you get up in the middle of the night to go to the bathroom, only to find that the canine occupant of the room has already gone to the bathroom. How do you know? Because you've stepped into a little puddle (or worse) and your socks are a trifle damp. Not pleasant.

But people who live with housetrained dogs don't need to worry about Wet Sock Syndrome. By taking their pooches to their potties before bedtime, owners ensure that when they head to their own potties, their socks will stay dry.

The Dogs Have One Less Way to Embarrass Their Owners

Dogs can display their bad bathroom habits at the most inconvenient times. When my Golden girl, Allie, was a puppy, my husband and I invited several couples over to our home for a dinner party. Of course, we also wanted to show off Allie, who had just joined our household and who, even at the tender age of 11 weeks, showed clear signs of becoming the great beauty she is today. Allie apparently wanted to show off, too — but not in ways that my husband or I had planned.

First, I emerged from the kitchen into the dining room just in time to see Allie sitting next to the table with the tablecloth in her mouth. One yank would be all that was needed for the china, silver, napkins, and crystal to go flying. I quickly grabbed a treat and offered it to Allie, who promptly relinquished the tablecloth to grab the goodie.

I was a little embarrassed that I hadn't anticipated Allie's table move, but our guests seemed to find it funny. However, the guests were probably a little less amused a few minutes later when Allie toddled over to a corner of the living room and, without further ado, proceeded to squat and anoint the carpet. Certainly, I was not amused. I was mortified.

Those events occurred 6-and-a-half years ago. Today, Allie is a grown-up girl, but she still has a puppy's sense of mischief. When we have company, I still have to watch that she doesn't perform a mortifying maneuver such as counter surfing, tablecloth grabbing, or hors d'oeuvre sampling. However, Allie's long been a house-training ace. That means I can count on her to do the doo only at the proper time and place — which gives me one less reason to be embarrassed when company comes over.

The Owners Know Right Away When Their Dogs Are Sick

Housetraining a dog requires a certain amount of observation on the part of the housetrainer. Decoding the dog's pre-potty behavior, settling into a consistent pattern of trips to the potty, and observing what the dog's poop and pee normally look like are all important components of housetraining success.

But even after your dog becomes a housetraining ace, those powers of observation are important. That's because when a dog changes his bathroom habits, he's often exhibiting initial signs of illness. By noticing such changes, you can detect the signs of a health problem early on — which usually results in a faster diagnosis and easier, more effective treatment.

The Dogs Have a Great Foundation for Further Training

In all likelihood, housetraining will be among the first — if not *the* first — set of lessons you attempt to teach your dog. The way you try to show her proper canine potty etiquette lays the foundation for the ways you try to teach her other lessons, such as coming when called, sitting when told to, and walking nicely on the leash. What you do now, in this most basic set of lessons, will probably set the tone for your relationship with your dog now and for years to come. For that reason alone, it's worth taking the time to do the job well — and persevering until you can truly declare victory.

Dogs and Owners Communicate Better with Each Other

Housetraining is really a cooperative effort. The dog needs to cooperate with the owner by refraining from pooping or peeing anywhere but in the potty area that the owner has designated. The owner needs to cooperate with the dog by making sure she takes the dog to the potty area whenever the dog needs to do his business.

Such cooperation requires communication between person and pooch. The dog discovers that when the owner asks a leading question — such as "Do you want to go out?" or "Do you need to go potty?" — a bathroom break will follow shortly thereafter. In all likelihood, he'll also find a way to tell the owner that he needs to go even before the owner asks that crucial question. For example, Allie goes to the back door of our home and gently taps the glass or scratches the door. My previous canine companion, Cory, bopped his leash with his nose. The owner learns to watch for these signals — and to grant the dog's request whenever that request occurs. (For info on signals that your dog needs to go out, see Chapter 8.)

Such communication and cooperation help build the bond between owner and dog. They lay the foundation for a long and happy life together — a life built on mutual respect, trust, and love.

The Owners Are More Likely to Keep Their Dogs

A visit to any animal shelter provides heart-rending evidence of what happens when the bond between dog and person is broken. Behind almost every dog in a shelter is a sad story of loss or abandonment. All too often, a relationship that started out with joy or hope ends up with the owner being disappointed and the dog facing euthanasia at the shelter or dog pound.

One common cause of a rupture in the bond between a dog and his person is the dog's bathroom behavior. In a study sponsored by the National Council on Pet Population Study & Policy (www. petpopulation.org), house soiling was the most common reason that owners surrendered their dogs to shelters when those owners cited a variety of reasons for relinquishing their dogs.

This doesn't have to happen. A little time, a little patience, and a little perseverance can get just about any dog to become a housetraining ace. Make that investment in your dog's future, and you up the odds that the two of you will have a long and happy life together.

Appendix

Other Helpful Pit Stops for Housetrainers

*T*his book is designed to tell you everything you need to know to help you and your canine housetrainee live in an accident-free world forevermore. But if you just can't get enough info about pooch potty protocol and doggie bathroom boo-boos, here's a boatload of additional information designed to quench your thirst for such knowledge. As you sample these materials, you'll find a lot not only about housetraining but also about many other important aspects of canine health and behavior.

Go Online

Not surprisingly, the Internet has countless sites devoted to the trials, tribulations, and triumphs that the process of housetraining entails, not to mention other aspects of understanding canine behavior. Here are some of the best:

✔ **Pet Connection:** This is the fabulous Web site that deals with anything and everything having to do with companion animals. It's maintained by *Good Morning America's* favorite veterinarian, Dr. Marty Becker, and pet writer extraordinaire Gina Spadafori, author of (among other works) Wiley's classic *Dogs For Dummies.* The Web site includes not only a blog that details important issues regarding animal care but also the archives from the Pet Connection column published by the Universal Press Syndicate. The archives are searchable, and they include at least six articles that cover both house-training basics and fine points. Visit the site at www.pet connection.com.

✔ **Association of Pet Dog Trainers (APDT):** This organization
conducts continuing education programs for dog trainers,
with a strong emphasis on reward-based (read: positive
reinforcement) training. Although the site is geared mainly
toward professional instructors, there's some good stuff here
for the average dog owner, including a trainer database that
allows the owner to search for a trainer in his or her local
area. The site also includes many articles from the APDT
newsletter, *Chronicle of the Dog*, including several that deal
with housetraining issues. Check it out at www.apdt.com.

✔ **Merck Veterinary Manual:** The Merck Veterinary Manual
is a marvelous online resource for those who own all kinds
of animals, including dogs. The online version includes a
detailed table of contents that catalogs symptoms and
ailments by bodily system, as well as a database into which
you can type a search term and, more than likely, get more
information about that search term than you could imagine.
Of particular note is a succinct yet detailed description of
canine elimination problems and how to solve them. Go to
www.merckvetmanual.com.

✔ **The Humane Society of the United States (HSUS):** This
humongous site not only deals with a vast array of animal
welfare and advocacy issues but also includes information
on a variety of pet care topics — including housetraining.
Because bathroom issues are a significant reason people
surrender their dogs to animal shelters, the concern of the
HSUS about this subject is more than understandable. To
find out more, go to www.hsus.org.

✔ **Zero Odor:** Veterinary behaviorist Dr. Nicholas Dodman of
Tufts University's Cummings School of Veterinary Medicine
swears by this product, which its manufacturers flat-out
guarantee will end pet odor problems. Of course, ending odor
problems is crucial to successful housetraining — because if
any odor or other residue of a doggie bathroom transgression
remains, your housetrainee can be guaranteed to go back
to the site of that transgression and perform an encore. I
haven't used this product myself, but if Dr. Dodman gives it
a thumbs-up, I'm thinking it's got to be good. See what you
think by visiting www.zopet.com.

✔ **UGoDog:** This site showcases a unique indoor dog potty
called, appropriately, the UGoDog. I'm including this site
here in the appendix not because I endorse the product but
because the site contains some good basic housetraining
information. That said, as indoor canine bathrooms go, it's
more stylish looking than newspaper and can accommodate
larger dogs than other indoor potties can. Case in point: My
70-pound Golden Retriever, Allie, walked onto the UGoDog

without hesitation when asked. Nevertheless, I maintain that indoor bathrooms are best suited to small or medium-sized dogs. For the company's own lowdown, head over to `www.ugodog.net`.

✔ **Secondnature:** This is the Web site maintained by Nestlé-Purina to showcase its dog litter product. The inclusion of this site in this appendix isn't an endorsement of Secondnature over any other dog litter product on the market. The site does, however, include some good basic information that anyone can apply to potty training a dog, regardless of the method used. Find out more by moseying over to `www.doglitter.com`.

Book 'Em!

This book probably tells you more about housetraining than you ever wanted to know. However, on the off chance that you don't think it does or (more likely) that you want to know how to teach your dog to do other things and keep him healthy, here are some great sources of additional reading:

✔ *Dogs For Dummies,* **2nd Edition, by Gina Spadafori (Wiley):** Just about the best all-around dog care book ever written. Spadafori answers pretty much every question a dog owner (or prospective dog owner) could ask. Great reference book — and a great read, too.

✔ *The Holistic Dog Book: Canine Care for the 21st Century,* **by Denise Flaim (Howell Book House):** As far as I'm concerned, this is the best explanation of holistic veterinary medicine for dogs out there. The book provides terrific, detailed descriptions of how holistic veterinarians view canine health and nutrition.

✔ *The Power of Positive Dog Training,* **by Pat Miller (Howell Book House):** Miller is one of the best positive reinforcement dog trainers in the United States — and in this book, she shows why. She offers a readily understandable explanation of the science behind positive reinforcement and an equally clear description of how to use that science to train your dog humanely and wisely.

✔ *Puppies For Dummies,* **2nd Edition, by Sarah Hodgson (Wiley):** Hodgson deals with all things puppy in this lavishly illustrated tome, and she includes a great chapter on housetraining.

Flip through These Mags

The art of housetraining, just like anything else that employs the principles of canine behavioral science, is constantly evolving — and often, magazines can provide more timely information about that evolution than books can. Pet magazines, unfortunately, come and go, but the titles listed here have been around for a long time and are likely to stay around for an even longer period.

- ✔ *AKC Family Dog* (American Kennel Club): For people who own purebred dogs but don't exhibit those dogs in conformation shows (such as the annual Westminster Kennel Club Dog Show), the AKC offers this award-winning quarterly magazine. The articles and columns here emphasize basic dog care and training — including housetraining — and integrating your dog into your life. The magazine is available by subscription only. To subscribe, visit the AKC Web site at www.akc.org/pubs/familydog or call 800-490-5675.

- ✔ *Dog Fancy* (Bowtie, Inc.): Probably the most widely read dog-oriented magazine in the United States, *Dog Fancy* is chock-full of leading-edge information about dog health, care, and training (including housetraining, of course). It also contains breed profiles and other interesting features. It's available on newsstands at book and pet superstores, or you can subscribe at www.dogchannel.com.

- ✔ *Whole Dog Journal* (Belvoir Publications, Inc.): Not only does this monthly newsletter report on trends in alternative medicine and holistic health care for dogs, but it also offers state-of-the-art advice about positive reinforcement training, including its application for housetraining. The editors pay special attention to nutrition, and the publication may be best known for its annual lists of the best and worst commercial dog foods — which can make a big difference not only in your dog's overall health but also in his daily offloads. Subscriptions are available online at www.whole-dog-journal.com or by phone at 800-829-9165.

- ✔ *Your Dog* (Tufts Media): Tufts University's Cummings School of Veterinary Medicine, one of the finest vet schools in the United States, publishes this monthly 24-page newsletter. Articles are written by journalists but incorporate the Cummings School's faculty's expertise in dog health and behavior. It's available only by subscription, by visiting www.tuftsyourdog.com or calling 800-829-5116.

Index

BUSINESS, CAREERS & PERSONAL FINANCE

**Accounting For Dummies,
4th Edition***
978-0-470-24600-9

**Bookkeeping Workbook
For Dummies†**
978-0-470-16983-4

Commodities For Dummies
978-0-470-04928-0

Doing Business in China For Dummies
978-0-470-04929-7

E-Mail Marketing For Dummies
978-0-470-19087-6

**Job Interviews For Dummies,
3rd Edition*†**
978-0-470-17748-8

**Personal Finance Workbook
For Dummies*†**
978-0-470-09933-9

Real Estate License Exams For Dummies
978-0-7645-7623-2

Six Sigma For Dummies
978-0-7645-6798-8

**Small Business Kit For Dummies,
2nd Edition*†**
978-0-7645-5984-6

Telephone Sales For Dummies
978-0-470-16836-3

BUSINESS PRODUCTIVITY & MICROSOFT OFFICE

Access 2007 For Dummies
978-0-470-03649-5

Excel 2007 For Dummies
978-0-470-03737-9

Office 2007 For Dummies
978-0-470-00923-9

Outlook 2007 For Dummies
978-0-470-03830-7

PowerPoint 2007 For Dummies
978-0-470-04059-1

Project 2007 For Dummies
978-0-470-03651-8

QuickBooks 2008 For Dummies
978-0-470-18470-7

Quicken 2008 For Dummies
978-0-470-17473-9

**Salesforce.com For Dummies,
2nd Edition**
978-0-470-04893-1

Word 2007 For Dummies
978-0-470-03658-7

EDUCATION, HISTORY, REFERENCE & TEST PREPARATION

African American History For Dummies
978-0-7645-5469-8

Algebra For Dummies
978-0-7645-5325-7

Algebra Workbook For Dummies
978-0-7645-8467-1

Art History For Dummies
978-0-470-09910-0

ASVAB For Dummies, 2nd Edition
978-0-470-10671-6

British Military History For Dummies
978-0-470-03213-8

Calculus For Dummies
978-0-7645-2498-1

**Canadian History For Dummies, 2nd
Edition**
978-0-470-83656-9

Geometry Workbook For Dummies
978-0-471-79940-5

The SAT I For Dummies, 6th Edition
978-0-7645-7193-0

Series 7 Exam For Dummies
978-0-470-09932-2

World History For Dummies
978-0-7645-5242-7

FOOD, HOME, GARDEN, HOBBIES & HOME

Bridge For Dummies, 2nd Edition
978-0-471-92426-5

**Coin Collecting For Dummies,
2nd Edition**
978-0-470-22275-1

**Cooking Basics For Dummies,
3rd Edition**
978-0-7645-7206-7

Drawing For Dummies
978-0-7645-5476-6

**Etiquette For Dummies,
2nd Edition**
978-0-470-10672-3

Gardening Basics For Dummies*†
978-0-470-03749-2

Knitting Patterns For Dummies
978-0-470-04556-5

Living Gluten-Free For Dummies†
978-0-471-77383-2

**Painting Do-It-Yourself
For Dummies**
978-0-470-17533-0

HEALTH, SELF HELP, PARENTING & PETS

Anger Management For Dummies
978-0-470-03715-7

**Anxiety & Depression Workbook
For Dummies**
978-0-7645-9793-0

Dieting For Dummies, 2nd Edition
978-0-7645-4149-0

**Dog Training For Dummies,
2nd Edition**
978-0-7645-8418-3

Horseback Riding For Dummies
978-0-470-09719-9

Infertility For Dummies†
978-0-470-11518-3

**Meditation For Dummies with CD-ROM,
2nd Edition**
978-0-471-77774-8

**Post-Traumatic Stress Disorder
For Dummies**
978-0-470-04922-8

**Puppies For Dummies,
2nd Edition**
978-0-470-03717-1

**Thyroid For Dummies,
2nd Edition†**
978-0-471-78755-6

Type 1 Diabetes For Dummies*†
978-0-470-17811-9

* Separate Canadian edition also available
† Separate U.K. edition also available

INTERNET & DIGITAL MEDIA

AdWords For Dummies
978-0-470-15252-2

Blogging For Dummies, 2nd Edition
978-0-470-23017-6

Digital Photography All-in-One Desk Reference For Dummies, 3rd Edition
978-0-470-03743-0

Digital Photography For Dummies, 5th Edition
978-0-7645-9802-9

Digital SLR Cameras & Photography For Dummies, 2nd Edition
978-0-470-14927-0

eBay Business All-in-One Desk Reference For Dummies
978-0-7645-8438-1

eBay For Dummies, 5th Edition*
978-0-470-04529-9

eBay Listings That Sell For Dummies
978-0-471-78912-3

Facebook For Dummies
978-0-470-26273-3

The Internet For Dummies, 11th Edition
978-0-470-12174-0

Investing Online For Dummies, 5th Edition
978-0-7645-8456-5

iPod & iTunes For Dummies, 5th Edition
978-0-470-17474-6

MySpace For Dummies
978-0-470-09529-4

Podcasting For Dummies
978-0-471-74898-4

Search Engine Optimization For Dummies, 2nd Edition
978-0-471-97998-2

Second Life For Dummies
978-0-470-18025-9

Starting an eBay Business For Dummies,3rd Edition†
978-0-470-14924-9

GRAPHICS, DESIGN & WEB DEVELOPMENT

Adobe Creative Suite 3 Design Premium All-in-One Desk Reference For Dummies
978-0-470-11724-8

Adobe Web Suite CS3 All-in-One Desk Reference For Dummies
978-0-470-12099-6

AutoCAD 2008 For Dummies
978-0-470-11650-0

Building a Web Site For Dummies, 3rd Edition
978-0-470-14928-7

Creating Web Pages All-in-One Desk Reference For Dummies, 3rd Edition
978-0-470-09629-1

Creating Web Pages For Dummies, 8th Edition
978-0-470-08030-6

Dreamweaver CS3 For Dummies
978-0-470-11490-2

Flash CS3 For Dummies
978-0-470-12100-9

Google SketchUp For Dummies
978-0-470-13744-4

InDesign CS3 For Dummies
978-0-470-11865-8

Photoshop CS3 All-in-One Desk Reference For Dummies
978-0-470-11195-6

Photoshop CS3 For Dummies
978-0-470-11193-2

Photoshop Elements 5 For Dummies
978-0-470-09810-3

SolidWorks For Dummies
978-0-7645-9555-4

Visio 2007 For Dummies
978-0-470-08983-5

Web Design For Dummies, 2nd Edition
978-0-471-78117-2

Web Sites Do-It-Yourself For Dummies
978-0-470-16903-2

Web Stores Do-It-Yourself For Dummies
978-0-470-17443-2

LANGUAGES, RELIGION & SPIRITUALITY

Arabic For Dummies
978-0-471-77270-5

Chinese For Dummies, Audio Set
978-0-470-12766-7

French For Dummies
978-0-7645-5193-2

German For Dummies
978-0-7645-5195-6

Hebrew For Dummies
978-0-7645-5489-6

Ingles Para Dummies
978-0-7645-5427-8

Italian For Dummies, Audio Set
978-0-470-09586-7

Italian Verbs For Dummies
978-0-471-77389-4

Japanese For Dummies
978-0-7645-5429-2

Latin For Dummies
978-0-7645-5431-5

Portuguese For Dummies
978-0-471-78738-9

Russian For Dummies
978-0-471-78001-4

Spanish Phrases For Dummies
978-0-7645-7204-3

Spanish For Dummies
978-0-7645-5194-9

Spanish For Dummies, Audio Set
978-0-470-09585-0

The Bible For Dummies
978-0-7645-5296-0

Catholicism For Dummies
978-0-7645-5391-2

The Historical Jesus For Dummies
978-0-470-16785-4

Islam For Dummies
978-0-7645-5503-9

Spirituality For Dummies, 2nd Edition
978-0-470-19142-2

NETWORKING AND PROGRAMMING

ASP.NET 3.5 For Dummies
978-0-470-19592-5

C# 2008 For Dummies
978-0-470-19109-5

Hacking For Dummies, 2nd Edition
978-0-470-05235-8

Home Networking For Dummies, 4th Edition
978-0-470-11806-1

Java For Dummies, 4th Edition
978-0-470-08716-9

Microsoft® SQL Server™ 2008 All-in-One Desk Reference For Dummies
978-0-470-17954-3

Networking All-in-One Desk Reference For Dummies, 2nd Edition
978-0-7645-9939-2

Networking For Dummies, 8th Edition
978-0-470-05620-2

SharePoint 2007 For Dummies
978-0-470-09941-4

Wireless Home Networking For Dummies, 2nd Edition
978-0-471-74940-0